D1136001

FAIRNESS FOR ALL

Unlocking the power of employee engagement

FAIRNESS FOR ALL

Unlocking the power of employee engagement

MARK PRICE

www.measuringworkplacehappiness.com

STOUR
PUBLISHING
An imprint of
David Fickling Books

Published in Great Britain in 2017 by Stour Publishing
An imprint of David Fickling Books

31 Beaumont Street,
Oxford,
OX1 2NP

www.davidficklingbooks.com

Copyright © Mark Price, 2017

Every effort has been made to trace copyright holders and
obtain their permission for the use of copyright material.
The publisher apologises for any errors or omissions and would
be grateful if notified of any corrections that should be incorporated
in future reprints or editions of this book.

The moral right of the author has been asserted.

British Library Cataloguing-in-Publication Data
A catalogue record for this book is available on
request from the British Library

ISBN 978 1 910989 22 7

Typeset in Minion Pro 11.5/17

Printed and bound in Great Britain by Clays Ltd, St Ives plc

MIX
Paper from
responsible sources
FSC
www.fsc.org
FSC® C018072

To Judith, who taught me that personal happiness comes from appreciating what you have.

CONTENTS

Foreword

Around a century ago, John Spedan Lewis had a brilliant and revolutionary idea about a different way to run a business. During a long convalescence following a nasty riding accident, he was struck by the injustice that he, his brother and father, John Lewis, earned more from their eponymous department store business than the rest of the staff put together. Using his own time off recovering to visit sick employees, he was shocked by their living conditions. Some say this led to his philanthropic act of putting the shares of the company into a trust for the benefit of all the employees once his father had died. Others say the swirling threat of communism that prevailed at that time led him to what he called 'Partnership for All' and 'Fairer Shares'. Whatever the motivations, the result was, and continues to be, a business run for profit, but one where the employees, or 'Partners', control the money, and not one, as is typical, where the sources of money control the employees: a business that explicitly sets out to balance and promote the interests of all stakeholders – employees, customers and suppliers – both to secure its long-term sustainability and for the benefit of society. Or as Spedan put it, 'the Partnership was created wholly and solely to make the world a bit happier and a bit more decent.'

John Spedan Lewis was an educated man with an enquiring mind and, like many Victorians, revelled in the natural world and the excitement created by the theories of Darwin and others. His passion for naturalism made him a keen observer, explorer and experimenter. I like to think this unique combination of attributes inspired him to share the rewards of success and responsibility of ownership with all in the company.

In his written constitution, he outlined that the first principle and supreme purpose of the John Lewis Partnership was the happiness of the employees, or Partners. He saw the commercial advantages of this approach long before others did: more engaged employees give better service, as a result of which customers will be more satisfied and therefore more loyal, which in turn leads to sustained profitability. After more than thirty years working in the Partnership, I came to see the wisdom of his extraordinary foresight for a modern world challenged by capitalism's extremes.

My father twice set up his own small business and, as a committed Christian and preacher, he held many similar values to Spedan Lewis. He taught me two valuable lessons. Firstly, that all people are born equal, but with different and unique skills and abilities. And secondly, that ripping customers off for a short-term benefit is not the recipe for long-term success. His guidance through my early years, and then my time working in Spedan's Partnership, have shaped my thinking, both in principle and practice, about what is now termed 'a fairer form of capitalism'. That thinking crystallised further as I travelled the world during my time as the UK government's Minister for Trade and Investment.

It was the tents and temporary shelters pitched outside St Paul's Cathedral, London, for five cold, wet months from October 2011 that stirred me to write this book to share Spedan's views in a modern context. The inhabitants of this new, ramshackle community were protesting about the negative impact capitalism and globalisation was having on their lives. On the several occasions I visited they didn't express their concern in those terms, rather that it didn't seem right to them that the rich were getting richer and the poor poorer, while at the same time they were losing their jobs to more lowly paid migrants, or to new technology or cheap labour overseas. They said they were not getting a fair return for their efforts, working harder to stand still at best, that politicians were disconnected from their plight and that institutions no longer served them well. So they reached out to the Church to hear their plight. One of the most striking things about this group was its diversity. They weren't the balaclava-disguised, missile-throwing, anti-capitalist protestors we are used to seeing on the TV, battling the police in the streets outside various world summits. They were ordinary people from Bury, Birmingham and Brighton, brought together by their heartfelt desire to make a change. To have jobs which rewarded them fairly, to be able to afford to buy property and have schools and hospitals able to meet their needs. Their compassion drew in the homeless, mentally ill and dispossessed. As a group they honestly felt they had nowhere else to turn. While Church leaders steadfastly held out against robust measures to end the very public protest, they did appear to struggle to respond in any meaningful way. In early spring, the protestors were finally persuaded to pack up their dwellings and move on. However, the problems didn't go away with them, and some would say they have become worse. As the now Archbishop of Canterbury, Justin Welby, said: 'Occupy reflects a deep-seated sense that there is something wrong, and we need to think very hard about what's wrong.' [1]

It's hard to disagree. The inescapable truth is that something has indeed gone wrong and it's not just in the UK. We have seen similar public unrest in the USA, Greece, Italy, Germany and Spain. Protests against global trade deals have become widespread across

[1] The Saturday interview: Justin Welby, *Guardian*, 21 July 2012

Europe in the Netherlands and Belgium, Austria and Germany, nations famed for their liberal free trade stance. Trade ministers across the developed world have repeated to me echoes from their own countries of the sentiments of those protesters outside St Paul's. This growing populist issue has been adopted by both far left and right-wing politicans and is gaining traction, with the many who are reaching for a better way. They clamour for greater equality, the chance to get into work, to progress, and to be able to afford their own homes. And their concerns are justified. According to Oxfam's 2015 global inequality report the 62 wealthiest people in the world own as much wealth as over half the rest of the world's population put together. Five years ago it was 368 people. And top executives, who earned 47 times more than their average employee around twenty years ago, now earn 183 times more.[2] What unites all these protestors is the belief that capitalism and globalisation are failing both them and society as a whole.

But these are not just the lone voices of the poor and

[2] 'Wealth: Having it all and wanting more,' Oxfam International, 19 January 2015

dispossessed. In recent years many prominent figures have added their weight to the argument that we can't go on like this. The gap between the haves and have-nots has become too large to ignore. Martin Luther King said he didn't want his children to grow up on 'a lonely island of poverty in the midst of a vast ocean of material prosperity', but it now looks more likely that, conversely, there will be islands of great prosperity in a sea of subsistence. Just look at the rise of gated communities.

As far back as 1990, Czech President Vaclav Havel, who had been proclaimed the people's hero for his part in defeating communism, warned that capitalism wasn't necessarily the answer either. In a passionate speech to US Congress, he argued: 'Without a global revolution in the sphere of human consciousness, nothing will change for the better in the sphere of our being as humans, and the catastrophe toward which this world is headed – be it ecological, social, demographic or a general breakdown of civilisation – will be unavoidable.' [3]

[3] http://vaclavhavel.cz/showtrans.php?cat=projevy&val=322_aj_projevy.html&typ=HTML, retrieved 29 January 2016.

On the presidential campaign trail a quarter of a century later, Hillary Clinton echoed the sentiment. In a strongly worded message to voters she declared that capitalism was failing. Wall Street had hijacked corporate America, she said, and shareholders' incessant greed for short-term profits was sucking business dry and robbing it of much-needed long-term investment. In Clinton's view, businesses are no longer spending money on re-equipping, research, training and innovation because they are too intent on dutifully pouring money back into investors' coffers. She wants a more equitable way of working, declaring that there is untapped potential in profit sharing and outright employee ownership.[4]

Her Republican opponent, Donald Trump, who became the 45th president of the United States of America, took a different but equally aggressive line. His rallying cry, 'to make America great again', was aimed at disenfranchised white voters in the rust belt and the Midwest. His campaign answer was more protectionism and an end to trade deals. Free trade, and with it globalisation, was losing its major

[4] 'Clinton Sets Out Her Faith in Profit-Sharing,' *Financial Times*, 15 July 2015.

exponent as ordinary Americans kicked back against a system they saw failing them.

Andy Haldane, the Bank of England's chief economist, issued a similarly robust message. The respected commentator took to BBC's *Newsnight* to lay out the figures: A company that a generation ago had, say, profits of £10, would have paid out £1 to shareholders and retained £9 to invest for the future. Today they pay out £6 and retain £4.[5] You don't need to be an economics expert to understand that this is unsustainable in the long term. Nor is it simply a 'business problem', or a symptom of the natural peaks and troughs of the free market. It is something none of us can ignore because sustained investment is not just essential for individual businesses, it is vital to economic growth and our prosperity as a nation. If companies don't put something back in, productivity doesn't improve, wages stagnate and the economy won't grow. No wonder so many people have lost trust in business and finance.

[5] 'Shareholder power "holding back economic growth",' BBC News, 24 July 2015.

Veteran business leaders echo the same conclusions. Lloyd's chairman John Nelson, now in his fiftieth year in the City of London, used a speech to identify a substantial 'trust deficit' in business that has serious implications, not just for the City, but for society as a whole.[6] He made an urgent call for businesses to rebuild this trust by demonstrating 'significant changes in behaviour' and returning to the true purpose of business: providing customers with the best possible service, in the way they want it, with integrity.

Successive governments have tried to tackle the issue. Margaret Thatcher, when British Prime Minister, talked about 'every earner being an owner', and building a society, rather than a class, of 'haves'. But over recent decades the distribution of shares and home ownership has fallen. More recently David Cameron also tried, first with his 'big society' drive to empower communities and encourage private investment and then, with a determination to root out inequality and unfairness and to open up opportunities, with the ambition for a

[6] https://www.lloyds.com/news-and-insight/press-centre/press-releases/2015/10/lloyds-city-dinner, retrieved 29 January 2016.

'small island to become an even bigger economy'.

It can be no surprise that following the Brexit vote for the UK to leave the EU in 2016 the new British Prime Minister, Theresa May, returned to the theme in her first speech outside No. 10 Downing Street. And again in her first party conference speech where she said '... the referendum was not just a vote to withdraw from the EU. It was about something broader – something that the European Union had come to represent. It was about a sense – deep, profound and let's face it often justified – that many people have today that the world works well for a privileged few, but not for them. It was a vote not just to change Britain's relationship with the European Union, but to call for a change in the way our country works – and the people for whom it works – forever. Knock on almost any door in almost any part of the country, and you will find the roots of the revolution laid bare. Our society should work for everyone, but if you can't afford to get onto the property ladder, or your child is stuck in a bad school, it doesn't feel like it's working for you. Our economy should work for everyone, but if your pay has stagnated for several years in a row and fixed items of spending keep going up, it doesn't feel like it's working for you. Our democracy should work for everyone, but if you've been trying to say things need to change for years and your complaints fall on deaf ears, it doesn't feel like it's working for you. And the roots of the revolution run deep. Because it wasn't the wealthy who made the biggest sacrifices after the financial crash, but ordinary, working class families. And if you're one of those people who lost their job, who stayed in work but on reduced hours, took a pay cut as household bills rocketed, or – and I know a lot of people don't like to admit this – someone who finds themselves out of work or on lower wages because of low-skilled immigration, life simply doesn't seem fair. It feels like your dreams have been sacrificed in the service of others. So change has got to come. Because if we don't respond – if we don't take this opportunity to deliver the change people want – resentments will grow. Divisions will become entrenched.'[7] Across the world the issue of a fairer form

7 http://press.conservatives.com/post/151378268295/prime-minister-the-good-that-government-can-do

of capitalism is not the sole preserve of the right or the left of politics, it has become populist, and clearly the calls to find another way are not going to go away.

The good news is that we don't need to look very far. There are other business models where the rewards are more evenly shared so that everyone benefits, be it workers, suppliers, customers or the wider community. One of the best known of these is the John Lewis Partnership, which has worked successfully for over a century. The basis of this model is inclusive capitalism, which is about getting people in work and on in work. Acting responsibly to all stakeholders is central to this theme, with employees, the most important stakeholders, the drivers of it all.

This book is about that other way. A fairer way. A sustainable way.

INTRODUCTION

It was a stiflingly hot summer day, made worse by drenching humidity which sapped the energy and made all senses feel dull and sluggish. Entering the lecture theatre at Columbus University Business School in downtown New York, along with thirty-nine other executives from around the world, we were grateful to find it pleasantly chilled. We slipped into the seats behind our neatly typed name cards and the hubbub of polite chatter subsided as the lecturer entered the room. The atmosphere crackled with anticipation. It was the start of a week-long intensive course and expectations were high.

When the lecturer reached the front, he greeted the class with a nod, then turned to the immense blackboard and picked up a piece of white chalk. Starting high up in the left-hand corner he spelled out a question in large, bold letters, the chalk squeaking under the pressure.

'What is the supreme purpose of chief executives?' he wrote. Hands shot up all around the lecture theatre. Pointing at a gentleman in the front row the lecturer simply said: 'Yes?'

'To maximise shareholder value,' came the confident reply. Heads around the amphitheatre-style room nodded vehemently in agreement. Other hands were raised and a volley of further comments quickly ensued. Each one was a variation on the theme with broadly the same meaning.

'Generate profit at any cost: eat or be eaten, it's the survival of the fittest.'

'If shareholders don't get the best return they will move their money from your business to another where they can do better. Then you are ruined.'

'Keep costs lean to maximise returns.'

The message was clear: these executives had to do everything in their power to drive short-term returns. Concern for the environment, for communities, for individuals seemed secondary. Perhaps this is an acceptable consequence of capitalism, a system that has achieved so much in other ways. The economist

Milton Friedman, who in 1970 wrote an article entitled 'The Social Responsibility of Business is to Increase Profits' and whose body of work provides an academic backbone for this approach, would have been very pleased.[8]

The lecturer nodded in approval, clearly pleased with the results of his opening gambit. 'Very good,' he said, preparing to move on.

I had heard this 'truth' many times before. I was told it at the London Business School in the mid 1990s, at INSEAD in Fontainebleau and at William and Mary University in Virginia, which ran a world-class executive retail programme. I didn't believe it on any of those occasions and I didn't believe it here in New York. This time was different though. This time I felt confident and informed enough to say something. Twenty years of experience working for the John Lewis Partnership had led me to a different answer, to a different 'truth'. It was a truth with humanity and longevity at its heart, one that valued and maximised the contribution of

[8] 'The Social Responsibility of Business is to Increase Profits,' Milton Friedman, *The New York Times Magazine*, 13 September 1970.

all stakeholders for the good of everyone, not just one small group of detached financiers. My truth was and is a fairer form of capitalism, an answer to the criticism of free trade and globalisation which has done so much to lift many from poverty. Calmly I raised my arm to attract the lecturer's attention just as he was turning back to the board.

'Yes?' he said, his expression giving away the fact that he was clearly wondering what else there was to say on the point. Everyone in the room had already covered it eloquently, in his view.

'To my mind, the supreme purpose of a CEO is to maximise employee happiness,' I began nervously. 'Happy employees give more, which means customers get more. Suppliers and communities all benefit as a result and so would shareholders.'

My comments lit a spark, and for a full week, through every scheduled module, we debated where capitalism brought good – political, civil and economic freedom – and where, in the pursuit of maximising profit, long-term harm could be done. A reflective mood struck us all: was it really right to catch all the fish in the ocean for today's consumers and leave nothing for the future? Or close a factory and in so doing destroy a community simply to exploit cheap labour in another part of the world? Or knowingly mislead customers into buying something that wasn't in their interests?

More than ten years on from that course, during which time I led Waitrose through the turbulent years following the global financial crisis of 2007/8, I believe more than ever that capitalism needs a different approach; a kinder, more thoughtful, tolerant, patient, engaging and inclusive approach. It needs to embrace the many, not the few, if it is going to survive as the world's prevalent economic force, and it needs to consider and weigh up carefully its long-term impacts on future generations.

And that's what customers say they want too. In research carried out by Conlumino for Waitrose:

- 51% believe business cares only about money and nothing else

- 56% say business culture is dominated by greed and selfishness

- 66% see business putting profit before the environment

- 61% agree staff are seen as 'resources' rather than human beings

Big business comes in for the most criticism: just over half the group surveyed (58 per cent) had respect for large companies, compared to 96 per cent who had good things to say for small companies.

Whose interests do you think businesses put first, second, third and so on? And whose interests should they put first?

The ranking of interests remains unchanged since the last wave. People still believe that businesses prioritise the interests of directors and top executives first, while putting local communities last. People believe that directors' interests should be put last.

	FIRST	SECOND	THIRD	FOURTH	FIFTH	SIXTH
The order in which people think businesses actually put interests	DIRECTORS AND TOP EXECUTIVES	SHAREHOLDERS AND INVESTORS	CUSTOMERS	GOVERNMENT AND REGULATORS	EMPLOYEES	LOCAL COMMUNITIES
The order in which people think businesses should put interests	CUSTOMERS	EMPLOYEES	SHAREHOLDERS AND INVESTORS	LOCAL COMMUNITIES	GOVERNMENT AND REGULATORS	DIRECTORS AND TOP EXECUTIVES

The positions are based on the average ranking people gave different types of groups in terms of how business proritises their interests.

Further research for Business in the Community/ IPSOS Mori in April 2015 showed that just a fifth of employees say they are proud to work for their organisation, and only 22 per cent feel good about their employer's behaviour towards society.

The issue of trust in business is not new; similar concerns are echoed throughout history. But perhaps the rise of social media has brought greater connectivity, transparency and discontent.

For the avoidance of doubt, I believe in free enterprise and wholly embrace the importance of wealth-creating businesses for the good of both the economy and society. I believe in taxes being paid directly and indirectly through the workforce and supply chain for the government to spend on society's needs. And I believe the vast majority of companies act responsibly. But we have a system in which, according to Milton Friedman's theory, corporate executives will 'conduct the business in accordance with their [the owners'] desires, which generally will be to make as much money as possible, while conforming to the basic rules of the society, both those embodied in law and those embodied in ethical custom'.[9] My experience of more than three decades in business is that constant new rules and regulations to correct abuse have not reduced the general concerns of the public, as the research I have shared (and more besides) demonstrates. The principle of capitalism in its purest form, and with it, free trade, is struggling for hearts and minds.

There seem to be three reasons for this: human frailty, government partiality and globalisation. Human frailty in corporate executives comes from a fear of not performing – and all that flows from that – and from greed. This is clear in the increased share of company profits now going to executives and shareholders. Or, as I set out later, significantly increased executive pay and examples like that of VW car technicians cheating emissions tests in the USA.

Government partiality is another issue. Governments, democratic and otherwise, are politically programmed to be parochial and act in the best interests of their constituents to retain power.

[9] 'Social Responsibility of Buisness,' Milton Friedman, *NYT Magazine*, 1970

They are susceptible to lobbying and procrastination. You only need to look at the annual European Union agreement on fish quotas to see the inherent challenges governments face in 'protecting' the interests of their own commercial fishermen whilst taking advice on conserving stocks. And even landlocked countries join the debate on one side or another! Or you might look at international climate change talks, and the different interests of developed and developing countries. How are those countries that contain the Amazon rainforest, the lungs of the world, compensated for protecting it for the world's benefit and not exploiting the forest commercially for their own benefit?

And then there is increasing globalisation. In 1950 the world's population stood at 2.5 billion. By 1980 it had reached 4.4 billion and a further thirty years on, in 2010, it had risen to 6.8 billion. Such huge increases have been accompanied by an increasingly connected world in which businesses have stretched their activities across continents. Both processes have led to greater pressures on the world's resources. At the same time, corporations have taken advantage of their global reach to legitimately exploit government rivalries and competition: to, for example, pay as little tax as possible in the most advantageous jurisdictions. It is a moral dilemma, Apple Inc for example has chosen to headquarter their European operation in the Republic of Ireland and legitimately, under Irish tax law, does not pay taxes on profits made in the rest of Europe. Apple corporate executives acted in the interests of their shareholders, a national government set an attractive tax rate to bring investment and jobs and globalisation allowed them to do it, bringing the current system into disrepute in the eyes of ordinary people. The European Commission are attempting to regulate by imposing a £10 billion fine for unpaid European corporation tax, but the Irish government is not keen to collect, and Apple is not keen to pay, feeling they have done nothing wrong, while the US government makes representations feeling one of their companies is being victimised. Apple is not the only company that has been targeted for securing favourable tax deals in the European Union.

Last year, the commission told the Netherlands to

recover as much as €30m (£25.6m) from Starbucks, while Luxembourg was ordered to claw back a similar amount from Fiat. The issue raises a number of questions. Should one company be made an example of? What is fair in this instance? And most importantly how can a fair global system be achieved? Thirty-seven corporations are now listed as having revenues large enough to place them in a league table of the top one hundred wealthiest nations, increasingly shifting power and influence from governments to multinationals. To my mind the G20 nations and the World Trade Organisation have a significant role to play in creating the framework for a fair and sustainable economic model.

As the Nobel Prize-winning economist Joseph Stiglitz said:

What is clear is the policies of the last third of a century have not worked. There was an effort to rewrite the rules of the market economy, changing corporate governing, changing the rules of globalisation, changing the rules of the financial market. The net effect of all this has been more short-sighted behaviour, lower growth and more inequality.[10]

They have also failed to address the growing concern of many that the distribution of wealth from business success is not fairly shared. As a result, I believe there needs to be morality and humanity in how businesses behave, underpinned and supported by governments in a mutually supportive contract. If business is given the conditions to flourish then in return it should embrace a wider responsibility to all stakeholders, including employees, customers, suppliers and communities. The way business acts towards those stakeholders is how it connects with society and wins trust and admiration. Business is a force for good. The majority of taxes collected by governments comes from businesses. Those taxes pay for schools, hospitals and our defence. The success of business and of society are inextricably linked. Capitalism, and with it trade liberalisation, is the right model, it has raised billions from poverty,

[10] Interview on BBC Radio 4 with Simon Jack on the Today programme, Tuesday 8th January, 2013

just look at India and China as examples, but it needs to be in a version that works better for the benefit of all – and perhaps a little more along the lines of co-owned businesses, such as Waitrose and the John Lewis Partnership.

Over my three decades working with the Partnership, latterly as Managing Director of Waitrose and Deputy Chairman of the John Lewis Partnership, people regularly asked me whether the Partnership's way of doing business could be replicated elsewhere. There has been even more interest following the financial crisis and subsequent recession.

There are some interesting parallels between the situation we have found ourselves in following the financial crisis, and the conditions that shaped the beginnings of the John Lewis Partnership following the First World War and subsequent Great Depression. The questions being asked then centred on the dangers of unconstrained capitalism and the growing divide between the well-off and the poor. Whilst governments were cash-strapped, there were similar rumblings of discontent about corporate greed and capitalism's desire to seek the best returns for shareholders irrespective of the consequences on communities. People looked for a different way and turned to the extremes of fascism, Marxism and communism. It was in this environment that John Spedan Lewis put the shares of his family business into a trust for the benefit of everybody who worked in the organisation. His declared aim was to create a better balance between the needs of all stakeholders.

John Spedan Lewis believed strongly that if all employees were given a share in profits, as well as information on how the company was doing and the power to influence its direction, it would be better for everyone. His contention that the natural consequence of this strategy was that customers would, in turn, feel more valued, and that commercial success would follow has been proved correct year after year. Thanks to this better and fairer way of working, the two successful trading businesses, Waitrose supermarkets and John Lewis department stores, have consistently remained buoyant, even in the face of a succession of the most crippling downturns.

Yet, for all the success and the widespread desire for a

better way of doing business, there seems little appetite to follow the Partnership's lead from shareholders of quoted companies, governments looking to privatise nationalised industries, or even family businesses wishing to preserve the financial benefit accumulated for future generations. Those who resist get bogged down with the idea that it's all about giving away stock to employees.

However, there are elements of how the Partnership operates that I believe are replicable and do not necessarily mean conceding ownership of an organisation. Incorporating just a few aspects of the model would help to make any business a little bit more decent, but also a lot more successful and sustainable. Replicating a great deal more could transform the ways companies are run and see benefits flow to workers, communities and society as a whole as well as shareholders.

I have already seen many elements of the Partnership philosophy successfully translated elsewhere during my four-year tenure as Chairman of Business in the Community, an organisation of which thousands of companies in the UK and internationally are now part.

The majority of organisations have introduced just a few principles, but they have managed to use them to powerful effect. In this group I would include Channel 4, Unipart, Timpson and a small number of NHS Trusts, to name but a few. Some businesses have fully embraced the positive effects of employee ownership, with more than a hundred UK companies now boasting this structure, including Blackwell's bookshops, jam maker Wilkin & Sons and polymers manufacturer Scott Bader. Elsewhere some companies are opting for something in between a 'Partnership Lite' model and full employee ownership. At the time of writing, the City accountancy firm Grant Thornton has announced a profit-sharing scheme that could boost employee pay by a quarter. There is also increasing evidence that employees in an internet-empowered age are pushing for a change towards a more inclusive, fairer and different way to do business.

In this book I have set out the founding principles of the Partnership and explained how employee engagement is the key to unlocking greater productivity, better performance, a more connected workforce and solid long-term results. I have described why the Partnership's focus on the happiness of its Partners (employees) is a powerful economic driver. It is also the driver behind customer satisfaction, because Partners are on the front line and happy employees really do equal happy customers.

But what of the wider calls for action to make business fairer? How does any of this help society as a whole? Well, in addition to an economic argument in favour of engagement to ensure companies perform better, I try to show how the Partnership's more inclusive approach makes for more sustainable business decisions that act in the interest of the wider community. I believe there is a moral imperative for employee engagement. Engaged employees drive ethical business practices. It is what matters to them and it is what should matter to the executives who head our companies. The simple message is; if you focus on your employees' well-being and happiness, you will do better and society will be better off too. Happiness is derived from a sense of ownership and control and feeling positive about the environment in which you work.

In part two of this book I describe the six elements that drive the happiness of employees and how they relate to business. Those elements are:

- Step One: Reward and recognition – Pay is important in any job, but linking it to recognition is a powerful motivator.

- Step Two: Information – An open, transparent culture ensures widespread understanding of objectives.

- Step Three: Empowerment – Once employees know what needs to be done, if you empower them they'll make intelligent suggestions on the best way to do it.

- Step Four: Well-being – A happy, healthy workforce is better equipped to do business.

- Step Five: Instilling pride – Pride in the workplace and its status in society adds to fulfilment.

- Step Six: Job satisfaction – A culture of trust and respect engages on a personal level and encourages a stronger bond.

Each of these elements controls our sense of happiness in what we do each working day and, in turn, ensures we give the best we have to get the job done. I also outline how you might measure happiness at work, and if you visit measuringworkplacehappiness.com, you and your organisation can get both quantitative and qualitative measurements.

The Partnership model is, as is well known, based on employee ownership and this is integral to its success. However, I have tried to show that elements can translate very successfully elsewhere, however your business is constructed. If employee happiness is the objective, it is possible to create a sense of ownership and responsibility around a business in a range of ways. Individuals who feel they have more power over their working life, well-being and environment will take more responsibility for the success of their employer.

This is not the costly option either. I am not calling

for businesses to invest millions to make their workers feel better for no discernible return. In fact, most of the measures outlined in this book need virtually no financial investment whatsoever, merely a change in approach. More importantly, engaging with employees will actually save companies money in the long term. It simply requires a new way of thinking.

One of the biggest criticisms of business is the focus on maximising short-term profit rather than investing for the long-term. Short-termism risks blighting so many companies today and can be damaging to the economy as a whole. Companies looking for a smooth flow of profits to satisfy shareholders may be less inclined to develop new innovations, build or buy newer machinery, or invest in their workforces because all of these expenses show up straight away on the balance sheet and reduce profits in the current quarter. The result of this short-term focus is to lower future output and competitiveness. Perhaps even more importantly, it reduces productivity.

There are signs that industry is beginning to recognise this increasing threat to our long-term prosperity. Paul Polman, the CEO of Anglo-Dutch consumer giant Unilever, says the short-term focus of current political and economic systems is failing us all and has spoken passionately about the need to become more in sync with society. After taking the bold step of moving away from quarterly profit updates, declaring he only wanted investors who were interested in supporting the long-term health of the company, he has launched a new model, which he calls 'sustainable and equitable' capitalism.[11]

Paul is one of a growing band of business leaders who recognise that corporations, indeed humanity, are heading for disaster unless we take a long-term view on the challenges of social injustice, climate change, resource scarcity and degradation of our ecosystems. It all starts with the way we treat the people who work for us. The most precious thing you can give someone, after your love, is your labour. Shouldn't that labour be prized rather than viewed as human capital to be exploited?

[11] 'Unilever's Paul Polman: Challenging the Status Quo,' *Guardian*, 24 April 2012

My firm desire is that this book opens the debate about a fairer form of capitalism and encourages boards, financiers and shareholders to stop for a moment to think: could we get better results if the focus was on employee engagement, rather than on maximising shareholder returns? I hope it makes managers stop and ask why those often described as the 'best managers' have the most engaged staff and achieve the best results. I hope it makes unions ask, what is their role in this more collaborative approach? I hope it makes employees ask, what is their responsibility in a more engaged workplace? To me, that would be a huge achievement. The endgame should be a more engaged society which promotes greater happiness, collective endeavour and a fairer sharing of success.

We all have a part to play in creating a fairer society: business, the consumer and the government. Making changes now will benefit us all in the long term and leave a worthwhile legacy for generations to come. That should surely be the supreme purpose of all chief executives, business leaders, politicians and the ordinary person on the street.

PART ONE

The Principle

CHAPTER ONE

Employee engagement

Employee engagement is the new battlefield for real competitive advantage

---

The Partnership's ultimate purpose is the happiness of all its members, through their worthwhile and satisfying employment in a successful business. Because the Partnership is owned in trust for its members, they share the responsibilities of ownership as well as its rewards: profit, knowledge and power.[12]

Spedan Lewis's foresight is enshrined in the Partnership's Principle set out above. He recognised that rewarding and holding employees responsible would drive increased engagement, which in turn

[12] John Lewis Partnership: Our Principles

would lead to commercial success.

One of the biggest clichés about business is that it is 'lonely at the top'. It is not uncommon to hear executives trot this one out and I often wonder if they have really thought about what they are saying. The only proper response to this assertion is: 'Why?' If you are alone, nobody is following you, and if nobody is following you then you are not leading. What kind of leader would leave anyone behind? An ineffectual one. An insecure one. A dysfunctional one. It simply doesn't make any sense for one person to shoulder the entire burden, to make every decision and command each action. An empowered team sees everyone playing rather than spectating.

It is instructive to look at the fortunes of major companies that were around when I joined the Partnership. The year, 1982, rather helpfully coincides with the date in which the Financial Times 100 Index first started, listing the top one hundred companies on the UK Stock Exchange by their capital value. More than thirty years on, only thirty-four of those original companies are still in the Index. Remember, at that time, these companies were perceived to be the *best businesses*, with the *best prospects* and, you would think, the *most effective management teams*. They also had the greatest amount of capital at their disposal. It wasn't enough.

Perhaps the most likely element missing from these companies was employee engagement, which when fully mobilised creates a personal self interest among employees in longevity and consistent growth. Share knowledge and information with employees, reward them for a job well done and encourage them to become fully immersed in the business and there is more chance a company will consistently prosper both in good times and in bad.

Think about it another way: imagine you are planning a holiday with your partner. Would you go home and say: we're going to Italy, to this hotel, from this date until this date? Or would you more likely settle down together around the table and flick through brochures, or compare findings online? The second option is not just more pleasurable for all concerned, but probably much more fruitful too because two heads are invariably better than one when it comes to solving issues.

There are very few scenarios in life where one party says: 'This is where we are going', leaving the other party to follow, having had no say in the process. In fact, the only real one is business. I often reflect on whether some businesses aren't run more along the lines of dictatorships or totalitarian states than democratic governments! Is it any wonder that some are accused of lacking trust and being disconnected from society? Or that employees don't feel engaged in what they do on a day-to-day basis and so don't deliver their maximum potential? At its worst, simmering resentment builds when there is little opportunity for expressing an alternative view, or a high personal risk in expressing an unpopular one, and this inevitably affects morale and engagement. I remember once having dinner with a charming lawyer who told me everyone in his chambers loved him and everything about their jobs. Things couldn't get better, he concluded. He was somewhat surprised when I listed all the requests I had to improve things in Waitrose. He had to confess that his view was based on his instincts, since there were no formal channels for employee feedback or involvement.

The most often-cited driver of employee engagement is employee ownership. In recent years there has been a surge of interest in employee-owned companies. The ranks are swelling at a rate of 10 per cent a year and the UK's top fifty employee-owned firms now contribute over £20 billion annually to the economy.[13] Two new tax-relief measures introduced by the government in 2014, the first of which grants company owners exemption from capital gains tax if they sell a controlling interest to an employee trust, and the second of which allows employees of such trusts a level of tax-free bonuses, will no doubt fuel this boom. Globally, many other developed nations are eyeing the potential upside of employee ownership as a new source of growth.

Even if companies are not prepared to go as far as giving away stakes there is a growing acceptance that the 'them and us' system that has long dominated business

[13] 'The Employee Ownership Top 50 2015,' Employee Ownership Association, 3 July 2015.

does not serve us all well. While the structures of many organisations, particularly the publicly owned ones, do not lend themselves to full Partnership-style ownership, there are plenty of examples of businesses that have adopted employee share schemes, where the wealth of workers is directly tied to workplace performance. Other firms have not made clear financial links, but follow practices similar to the Partnership, such as employee committees or workplace teams to help management decision-making. Whatever the chosen strategy, businesses that operate in this way all appear to agree that fostering closer, more democratic links with their teams leads to the entire company reaping the rewards. Evening out the inequalities of power that dog many organisations benefits the working environment, company culture and the bottom line.

If you look, there are plenty of examples of how powerful employees can be, given half the chance to have an input. Take Northern Gas Networks. The energy supplier started an employee empowerment programme in 2012, after an internal survey found people had no sense of loyalty or belonging to the company. The poll coincided with an external report that found low levels of customer satisfaction. Management launched an Inspire programme, which informed the team about the business strategy and then asked: what ideas have you got? Employees were actively encouraged to take ownership of the company and find solutions to challenges. Within three years the company won a number of awards for customer satisfaction, employee engagement and inspirational leadership.

Channel 4 has some similarities to the Partnership, even though it is not employee owned. As a television station, it has the benefit of a large pool of talented people who want to work there. However, like all public-service broadcasters, its budget is limited, so their rates of pay are not exceptional. What it does offer is a remarkable place to work, where individuals can feel a sense of pride in what they make. This pride is nurtured through a number of Partnership-style staff-development initiatives, including one to enable 360-degree feedback from the team (seniors, peers and juniors), numerous learning and development opportunities and a living commitment to equality and diversity. Employee engagement is evident in the high standard of everything the channel does.

To put it succinctly: if you invest more in your people, you will have a better business. Give something back to your team and they will give back to you. Engaged employees behave differently: they take responsibility for their careers and success; they own their engagement with pride and enjoy being a driving force.

Or, to look at it from the other side: what do disengaged employees do? They generally fall into two camps. The first is made up of individuals who are not just unhappy at work, but actively unhappy. In their intent to act out this unhappiness, they may well drive away customers, or monopolise a manager's time. They'll be less interested in solving problems or innovating. The second group is less overt, yet still equally damaging. They are not hostile, or disruptive, but only ever do just enough to get by. They are not particularly interested in getting involved with customers, or in any other aspect of the day-to-day business, such as productivity, profitability, safety or quality.

There will be many people reading this now who

might be thinking this is just 'touchy feely' stuff, which is all very well when times are good, but when it comes down to it, we've all got a job to do and should be getting on with it the best we can. Perhaps there may be a feeling that engaging with employees takes too much time away from 'real work'. Nothing could be further from the truth. There are sound and compelling reasons to engage your workforce. It *will* make a noticeable difference to your profitability, and in a range of different ways. Employee engagement is an emotional commitment an employee has to an organisation and its goals. When employees are engaged, they care and use discretionary effort. Fully engage your workforce and you will benefit from the following.

Increased productivity

Gallup, which has been measuring employee engagement for many years, suggests a 20 per cent or better boost to productivity and profitability for companies with high engagement. In such companies, shrinkage was down (28 per cent lower than their less engaged counterparts elsewhere), there were fewer safety incidents (48 per cent) and defects were lower (41 per cent).[14] There was a defined benefit to the balance sheet too. Companies with engaged workforces experienced 147 per cent higher earnings per share.

This point is not first on the list of benefits by accident. Productivity, or output per worker, has been identified as a key driver of growth in real incomes and of economic demand. In a speech in June 2015, Sir Jon Cunliffe, Deputy Governor of the Bank of England, said that while UK economic growth at 2.5 per cent was stronger than most of its G7 partners, productivity was 'dismal'.[15] Output per hour in the UK was 17 percentage points below the average for the rest of the major G7 advanced economies in 2013, the widest productivity gap since 1992. On an output per worker basis, UK productivity dropped to 19 percentage points below the rest of G7.[16]

[14] 'State of the American Workplace,' Gallup, 20 June 2013

[15] Sir Jon Cunliffe, Automotive Fellowship International dinner, 22 June 2015.

[16] 'Statistical Bulletin: International Comparisons of Productivity – Final Estimates 2013,' Office for National Statistics, 20 February 2015.

The UK has only grown so strongly in recent years by using spare labour supply from the post-credit-crunch stock of unemployed workers. Employment in the UK is now at its highest rate since records began in 1971. This means that now we are close to the end of that labour supply, it is vital that productivity growth picks up if the economy is to continue to grow robustly. In other words, productivity is *the* new challenge. If employee engagement has been proven to improve productivity, and it has, we owe it to ourselves to explore this option seriously.

—— Revenue, profit and shareholder returns ——

Company accounts traditionally show the workforce as a cost on the profit-and-loss statement, rather than an investment. This can encourage the one-dimensional line of thought that they are 'human resources', ignoring the people dimension entirely. But if you are wedded to the profit-at-all-costs principle, there are a few interesting statistics to consider.

Companies that engage their workforces deliver a better business performance and return to shareholders.

One survey found that companies that consistently delivered double-digit growth had employees who were more confident in their organisation's future, were happy they had the information they needed to do their job well and, understood the company goals and how they could contribute.[17] The report further found that in companies where 60 to 70 per cent of employees were engaged, average shareholder return was 24 per cent, while companies with only 40 to 60 per cent engagement saw shareholder returns of 9 per cent and companies with engagement below 25 per cent suffered negative returns. Other research has shown that businesses with highly engaged employees consistently beat average revenue growth in their sector by 1 per cent, while those with low engagement fell below the average by 2 per cent. A 5 per cent increase in total employee engagement equates to a 7 per cent increase in operating margin.[18]

[17] 'Employee Engagement Higher at Double-Digit Growth Companies,' Research Brief, Hewitt Associates, 2004, www.hewitt.com.

[18] '2012 Global Workforce Study,' Towers Watson, towerswatson.com.

Resilience

Businesses with a high level of staff engagement perform better during economic downturns. Employment increased more than 12.9 per cent in employee-owned businesses between 2008 and 2009, compared to only 2.7 per cent in other business models in the same period.[19] In organisations where there is a high focus on employee fulfilment, employees take a long-term view. Workers not only stay where they are for longer, but the evidence shows that engaged workers, who buy into what their organisation is about, also actively try to make a difference to get things back on track. Retaining this motivated and committed talent can prove invaluable when executing longer-term growth plans, and also leads to a significant advantage in business performance. The opposite is true of workers who are not fully engaged. Indeed, Gallup found that when economic conditions are tough, disengaged employees opt to 'wait around' to see what happens. They either tread water, becoming a lazy drag on

[19] 'The Employee Ownership Advantage,' Cass Business School, Department for Business Innovation and Skills, July 2012.

resources, or at worst become a disruptive force.

When it comes to working through difficult times, adding new customers to the current base is a key growth activity. Attracting and retaining new customers requires higher levels of employee commitment and initiative. Research shows that businesses with some level of employee ownership perform better, particularly those in the professional service sectors.[20]

————————— **Retention and absenteeism** —————————

Engaged employees are loyal and often cite job satisfaction as one of their main reasons for staying with an organisation. Although the retail sector is notorious for its high staff turnover, the Partnership's annual rate is markedly lower. Comparable businesses have rates of double or more. Elsewhere in the UK jobs market, staff turnover averages 15 per cent, and is expected to rise to 18 per cent by 2018. Globally, the figure is around 21 per cent, forecast to rise to 23 per cent by 2018.

To put this into context, the going rate for replacing

[20] 'The Employee Ownership Advantage,' Cass Business School, *op. cit.*

a mid-management employee is about 150 per cent of their salary. Entry-level employees' replacement costs range between 30 and 50 per cent, while specialists can cost up to 400 per cent of their salary to replace.[21] Any strategy that means a business can hang on to staff will save money, as well as ensuring continuity and efficiency.

Engaged staff stay longer too. The UK has one of the shortest average job tenures in the OECD,[22] which is down in part to the dynamism of our labour market. According to the Employee Outlook survey,[23] 23 per cent of respondents were looking for a new job with a different employer. Younger employees are more likely to be job-hunting than their older colleagues. The average tenure of a UK employee (taking out students from the list) is nine years. At somewhere like Waitrose, that figure is nearer ten.

[21] American Express.

[22] 'Megatrends,' Chartered Institute of Personnel and Development, July 2013

[23] 'Employee Outlook,' Chartered Institute of Personnel and Development, Spring 2015.

Engaged employees also take fewer sick days: an average of 2.69 sick days a year compared with 6.19 days for disengaged employees.[24] Businesses are putting themselves at risk and damaging the economy as a whole because millions of workers are not delivering to their full capability. Absenteeism costs UK businesses more than £31 billion every year, with sickness accounting for 90 per cent of that bill. It puts Brits at a disadvantage in the global marketplace too. UK workers take an average of 9 days off a year, which is considerably more than their counterparts in Australia (2.2 days) and USA (4.9 days).[25]

Stress at work, which leads to long-term absence, has more than doubled since the 1990s, with an estimated 500,000 suffering from work-related stress in the UK. Meanwhile, only a third of workers receive support to manage workplace stress.[26] Workers who

[24] 'Employee Engagement: How to Build a High Performance Workforce,' Gallup.

[25] 'The Rising Cost of Absence,' PricewaterhouseCoopers, 15 July 2013, pwc.co.uk.

[26] 'Health and Safety Statistics 2014/15,' UK Health and Safety Executive, www.hse.gov.uk/statistics.

feel demotivated with, or disengaged from, their work, or who find their working day stressful, are more likely to move on to pastures new. Not only are they less resilient to pressure, but they also feel less attached to the company where they work.

Confidence in leadership

Confidence in leadership has been identified as one of the most consistent predictors of employee engagement and commitment. When good leadership is in place, it can be felt throughout the entire organisation and leads to high morale, good employee retention and sustainable, long-term success. If employees don't feel engaged and are uncertain about leadership they'll have no idea how they fit into the bigger picture, or their level of importance in making it happen. Internal surveys show confidence in Waitrose's leadership running at more than 80 per cent along with satisfaction with the organisation. I remember sharing these figures with the chairman of a blue chip travel business. He turned to me and said: 'If we got 40 per cent for confidence in leadership, I'd be running around the room, punching the air and shouting with joy.'

To summarise all these effects: Highly engaged employees get results with energy, passion and purpose. They stick around longer, engage with customers with more enthusiasm and execute their daily tasks more reliably. They are your hidden weapon when it comes to growth in tough times because they hold the key to a more positive customer experience and improved productivity.

Employee engagement is not a 'soft' option. It is a hard business metric that has a measurable impact on the bottom line. Engaged employees trust their organisation to do its best by them and vice versa. It is a two-way process, as illustrated by the following case study.

CASE STUDY

In recent years, Waitrose moved its shop operations from a department-based approach to work content. This meant, for example, that instead of having seven separate departments planning replenishment there would be just one. This resulted in a significant reduction in management numbers to align with the new strategy. Partners were given careful explanations of what was happening and why, and the advantages expected to be achieved with the new structure. This was coupled with a detailed presentation of the growth plan and Partners were invited to comment and contribute. Because of the measured way it was done, with extensive trials and feedback, the process took nearly three years, but at the end of this time just five out of the five thousand managers who were potentially affected left the business, and it was possible to redistribute this valuable resource elsewhere in the company.

Contrast this outcome with the experience of another major retailer. This publicly traded organisation also decided upon a strategy that would see the removal of an entire tier of store managers. Their approach was very different though. An announcement was made to the stock market that the jobs of a number of store managers were to be 'redefined' and redundancies were anticipated. Within six months, two thousand out of five thousand managers in this tier had left the business. The chances are that the most competent workers would have dusted off their CVs and moved on within days of the announcement. Either way, this organisation lost two-fifths of its talented and trained workforce with barely a backwards glance. Between them these employees had thousands of hours of experience and knowledge. Meanwhile, rebuilding trust and motivation with those left behind cannot have been an easy job.

As the case study demonstrates, to get the best out of people, a business needs to show them as much commitment as they expect them to give in return. Trust and shared responsibility are the keys to success.

There has never been a better time to focus on employee engagement because our workforces face threats from a number of sources. The structure of the employer/employee relationship has changed dramatically over the past few years. While 'jobs for life' were consigned by many to the history books a long time ago, we have seen a further significant shift in the other direction. Zero-hours contracts, subcontracting, temporary contracts, part-time agreements: nonstandard employment, such as that offered by Uber, is the new standard and this makes two-way communication a challenge. Firms have become ever more inventive in ways to create flexibility for themselves while weakening the opportunity for workers to be engaged in creating mutual success. Some large companies, as well as numerous start-ups, have fully embraced subcontracting as the perfect way to get labour on demand. The argument goes that it is great for workers too because they benefit from fantastic job flexibility and can build their job around personal schedules. In some cases this is true. However, the other way of looking at it is that workers have dramatically less power in these flexible arrangements – it can be extremely stressful and play havoc with family budgets.

How can these arrangements lead to workers feeling engaged and involved in a company's success? How can your thoughts and ideas on improving something be garnered if you don't even know when you will be working next? And consider for a moment the impact on society as more people feel less connected and engaged with their employer and its role in their community. Perhaps we should reflect again on what is so wrong with the notion of a 'job for life'? Would a commitment by employers to retrain and reskill lead to a more confident and secure workforce and society?

There are, of course, further contemporary challenges. Technology is transforming the way we work. Computer automation of routine tasks means a single worker can now do the work that used to be done by dozens. The work is usually highly skilled and the government anticipates growth in highly skilled, white-collar occupations and further job losses for both skilled and semi-skilled manual roles and administrative, clerical and secretarial jobs.[27] You are five times more likely to have your job replaced by automation if you earn less than £30,000 than if you earn more than £100,000. Changes to the job market such as this, coupled with increasing turnover of employees, reduce the incentive for firms to invest in their employees. This too will have an effect on productivity.

[27] 'Working Futures 2012–2022,' Evidence Report 83, UK Commission for Employment and Skills, March 2014.

In the UK, the proportion of workers enrolled in education, or receiving training, fell by 3.8 per cent from 2010 to 2013, which is one of the biggest drops in Europe.[28] Firms *expect* relationships with workers to be shorter because well-trained workers will be in demand and quickly move on. The net result becomes a self-fulfilling prophecy: individuals don't receive the training and support they need, so they move on. Everyone is in a weaker position because of it.

All of these trends push corporate companies into ever more short-term working practices. Meanwhile, productivity is under constant threat at a time when high employment and stagnating wages mean rates of output are more important than ever before. If we wish to enjoy increased economic growth as a country, we need to focus on increasing output per worker. Higher productivity will play a major role in strengthening public finances. If we don't achieve this goal, the alternative is further damaging cuts to public spending and investment.

[28] 'Report on the Commission on Inclusive Prosperity', Center for American Progress, 15 January 2015, www.americanprogress.org

All the signs are that we need to turn the traditional business model on its head. This doesn't mean communism, or giving up on the profit model altogether. The John Lewis Partnership is a consistently profitable organisation and has been for many years. The difference is one of focus: on the happiness of employees, which means thinking deeply about their continued employment through retraining and redeployment, and on taking the long-term view, which translates into a stronger business that generates sustainable and sufficient profits.

Employee engagement is about establishing a mutual respect between employer and employee, which will equally serve all and make the business more profitable in many different ways. Even a small shift in focus will make a difference. At present, just 13 per cent of global workers say they are engaged in their jobs,[29] which leaves a lot of room for improvement.

We have an opportunity to better utilise our human potential. For many, this will entail a shift to a new way

[29] 'State of the Global Workforce,' Gallup, 8 October 2013.

of thinking, but firms that put their employees first will get a better result, both for themselves and the wider economy. It is not only perfectly possible to have huge commercial success if you focus on people first, it is a proven strategy to improve customer satisfaction and loyalty.

Chapter two

Customer satisfaction and loyalty

Can only be delivered by engaged employees

The Partnership aims to deal honestly with its customers and secure their loyalty and trust.[30]

Spedan Lewis's experiment in industrial democracy has an impact on the way in which the business is commercially run in a number of ways. As individual performance is rewarded with merit, as well as market-rate pay increases, the best are recruited and retained. Annual bonuses are paid from profits collectively earned, and awarded as a percentage of each individual's pay, so everyone works for each other to the benefit of the customer. The team trumps the individual. As a result, there are no individual sales

[30] The John Lewis Partnership: Our Principles

bonuses based on hitting targets. This means selling Partners give impartial advice designed to bring the customer back time and time again, rather than working to make a quick unsatisfactory sale. There are no quibbles over refunds for the same reason. All that is asked is that Partners use their best judgement to satisfy the customer and do the right thing for the long-term benefit of the business. It's a powerful, different and very successful approach. It's one that is proven to build trust with customers. Supporting this is a mantra that the most important customers are the ones you already have. Look after them well and new ones will follow through their recommendation. The approach echoes a commitment to current employees rather than a hiring-and-firing culture.

Not surprisingly, therefore, I am often asked to speak to companies about how they can improve their customer service. The request invariably comes from companies that describe themselves as 'customer centric' or as 'having a passion for customer service', but often can't get to where they want to be. My response is always the same: start by understanding what good service means to your target customers. Say, for example, a customer pops out in their lunch hour to buy a greetings card. Typically they'll want to find the card easily, with the design they want for a specific occasion. Provided the selection is good, their other criteria will be that the product is in stock and ready to take right away, no queuing, and fast till service with little or no chatting. Price is not really an issue, nor do they want a detailed description of how the card was made. If that same customer is buying a computer, they will want almost the reverse: lots of advice and keen pricing. If the item the customer chooses is out of stock they'll be happy to wait, but they'll have high expectations of after-sales support and an acknowledgement from the salesperson that they have spent a significant sum.

Once a business clearly understands what matters to its customers, it needs to be precise about how that standard is achieved and measured, so that it can be communicated to the team that needs to deliver this ideal. I once asked a manager of a gift department what his standard was for that department. It is, of course, essential that these areas are attractively presented for customers. 'To be neat and tidy,' he replied confidently. 'What does that mean?' I pressed. He shrugged his shoulders and clearly had no idea. I challenged him that if he couldn't explain it to me, how on earth could his team achieve this standard, let alone allow their performance to be measured.

Once you are clear about the elements of service that customers value, and have defined how to achieve and measure them, that is when the challenge really begins. Consistency is key. What makes companies brilliant at customer service is achieving the desired standard day in, day out. And, when it does go wrong (and it will), being brilliant in recovery.

Ask anyone to tell you a great customer service story about John Lewis or Waitrose and I wager that nine out of ten times they will tell you about something that went wrong, but was brilliantly put right. A big part of engaging a team is giving them the flexibility and confidence to act on their own initiative and, as the anecdotes show, they are pretty good at it. It is to their credit that the Partnership scores so highly in customer service surveys and wins countless awards.

Their initiative is the foundation for confidence in the business. If you can do that again and again, for decades, you will build trust.

So how is it done? The only way to achieve consistently good service standards is to think about the happiness of your employees. Firstly, your shining lights have to be motivated to stick around long enough for the benefit of their experience to be felt by customers and new recruits, and for a culture of great service to build. Retention is key. Secondly, employees need to feel engaged enough to want to deliver every day.

The balance of power between supplier and customer has shifted completely. Thanks to new technology, customers don't just have more information about the things they buy and a wider choice than ever before, but they can also voice any dissatisfaction *very* loudly indeed. The old maxim that an unhappy customer will tell a dozen or so of their friends no longer holds. Thanks to social media, thousands of people get to hear about it if your service is under par and they *will* act on this intelligence. More than one-third of those with access to the internet in the UK say they have chosen not to buy a product as a result of online comments from customers or other private individuals.[31] Online giants, such as Amazon and eBay, have helped take this new supplier/buyer dynamic one stage further by actively encouraging customers to post feedback on both the product *and* the service provided. This has now become the norm. If you are not looking after your customers properly, there really is nowhere to hide.

This shift in balance has irrevocably raised the bar in customer-service standards: expectations are far, far higher than they have ever been. Customers want the best possible price, with impeccable service, all delivered with honesty, integrity and total transparency, twenty-four hours a day, seven days a week. They also have a growing interest in environmental and social responsibility and will rate your company according to its performance in the wider community because, thanks to greater mobility, customers are increasingly recognising they are part of a larger, global marketplace

[31] 'Understanding Customer Relationships,' Alex Bollen and Claire Emes, Ipsos MORI, May 2008.

and want to see fair play. As if all this isn't tough enough for any business to get right (and don't forget you need to get it right every time, with *every single* customer), the customer service bar will just go on rising. No matter how great your product or service is today, your customer will want it to be even better tomorrow. Doing things the way they have always been done is not an option. The pressure is on to engage with customers and connect with them in a personal and memorable way.

As far back as 1976, the American Technical Assistance Research Programs Institute (TARP) showed that effective customer service and complaint handling made a crucial contribution to corporate profitability. Since then, a number of eminent business thinkers have explored the relationship between customer expectations of service, satisfaction and increased profits. Business author Tom Peters, Aldi founder Karl Albrecht and Harvard business logistics professor James L. Heskett are just a handful of well-known names who have all advocated superior service quality as the key to competitive advantage. In 1990, Harvard business experts Fred Reichheld and Earl Sasser put numbers to the value of customer loyalty after their study found that the longer a customer stays with a business, the more profitable they become. Reducing customer defections by just 5 per cent per annum can produce profit increases of between 25 per cent and 85 per cent, depending on your industry.[32] To put this into context, it is not uncommon in some sectors to lose 15 to 20 per cent of customers each year. Cutting defections in half could more than double the average company's growth rate. Plus, it is a self-perpetuating system: customers who receive great customer service are more loyal. Indeed, so much so, they do part of your job for you because they become advocates, recruiting friends and family. And those advocates are more trusted than any marketing message you send out.

While many businesses would say they agree wholeheartedly that customer service is a priority, the truth is that it is not always *the* priority. For most major

[32] 'Zero Defections: Quality Comes to Services,' Frederick F. Reichheld and W. Earl Sasser, *Harvard Business Review*, September–October 1990, hbr.org.

organisations, and publicly traded ones in particular, the order of focus can be:

1. Shareholders
2. Customers
3. Employees

One of the many perils of being a business that fixates on external shareholder returns is that when times get tough it is very tempting to cut back a little on what is given to the customer so the dividend is not compromised. Staff might also be trimmed with the view that those that are left can work a little harder to close the gaps. This is a very short-sighted view. Customers are no fools and no one should treat them as if they are. If you narrow everything down to the ultimate goal of giving a return to investors, you risk losing customers, which will erode the very profit you seek to retain. As the statistics above show, get customer service right and profits will follow. The key to keeping customers happy lies in your team. This list should be reversed.

I'm not alone in this thinking. Sir Richard Branson, who built Virgin into a global brand on the reputation of unrivalled commitment to customers, has come out publicly to say employees are actually his number-one focus.[33] Branson has, quite correctly, noted that if an individual is not appreciated, then they won't do things with a smile. If they don't treat employees well, companies risk losing customers over bad service. Indeed, it is Virgin policy to prioritise employees first, customers second and shareholders third. Branson's reasoning is that shareholders will do well, the customers will do better and the team will remain happy.

Even if some businesses accept focusing on customer service over and above pure profit as a priority, they often question the advantage of building a company around employees, versus around the customer. After all, if customer service is paramount and increasingly so, doesn't it make sense to concentrate on wowing the people who give you money? I have certainly noticed

[33] 'Richard Branson: Companies Should Put Employees First,' Oscar Raymundo, *Inc.*, October 2014, www.inc.com.

a growing tension in business in recent years about which strategy is more effective.

A number of big businesses have clearly chosen the customer-led route where the user's needs are at the centre of their organisation. Every action is taken with a view to understanding a customer's wants, needs and dislikes and finding the best possible way to deliver a ground-breaking experience. The Holy Grail is creating value to delight customers by inventing products or services customers didn't even know they wanted.

The Partnership's strategy comes at it from a different angle where, once again, Partners are at the centre. They are entrusted with the task of delighting the customer. To understand why this is effective, it is worth going back a stage and asking: what drives customer satisfaction? The John Lewis Partnership view is that it is much more than getting the 'best deal'. After all, while customers are cost conscious, they don't always go for the cheapest possible product. This is why high-end manufacturers thrive in all industries. In my experience, what drives customer satisfaction at Waitrose includes the following.

A fresh perspective and new ideas

Customers like their suppliers to bring something new to the table – literally in this case.

Delivering value

Sadly the word 'value' is now used in place of cheap. Value is the equation:

quality + service + price = value.

A willingness to collaborate

Customers want you to work with them to achieve their goals by being responsive to their concern and needs.

A personal connection

Ultimately, whether it is a supermarket or a high-end technology solution, every selling situation involves a connection between two individuals. People prefer to buy something from someone they like. They like you to remember them too, which is why staff retention is so important.

What single factor connects each of these points?

The human being who is doing the selling. Whether he or she is listening to feedback, or suggestions for a better way of doing things, working with a customer to help them find what they need, or simply giving them the time of day, good customer service comes from the employee on the ground.

I've always rather liked the old story about a janitor at NASA at the peak of the space race. He is asked by a group of visiting reporters what he does.

'I'm putting a man on the moon,' he replies.

And he is. Everyone within an organisation plays a vital role in making the business bigger, better and stronger. It doesn't matter how far you embrace new technology, or how successful your business is at the leading edge of innovation; we're not working towards a brave new world where human beings are no longer required. In fact, exactly the opposite. The role of employees in a modern organisation is more important than ever. They are its human face and the main point of contact with the customer. Try resolving a problem with Microsoft and then Apple and you'll see the difference human interaction still makes. To put it simply, happy employees help create happy, loyal customers, which ultimately benefits company profits.

A Waitrose cashier who speaks to three hundred customers in a day is just as important as a branch manager. If they are not brilliant with every one of those customers, the business will be weaker as a consequence. Just a simple smile and a 'Thank you for shopping with us today', makes all the difference to how a customer feels when they leave the store. Similarly, one of the aims of the Waitrose Community Matters scheme, where customers are given a token at the checkout to post for one of three good causes when they leave the supermarket, was to make customers leave feeling good about themselves.

Customers may welcome innovations, but they still want to see employees who clearly enjoy their jobs. Indeed, 77 per cent are more likely to 'believe a company offers a good quality product or service' if employees seem happy.[34] The obvious challenge is: how do you inspire your team to truly engage with customers? As a business, you can organise dozens of innovative

[34] 'Understanding Customer Relationships,' Alex Bollen and Claire Emes, Ipsos MORI, May 2008.

customer service initiatives, but they are only ever as good as the person who delivers them. Waitrose, for example, has installed concierge-style desks in all stores to welcome customers, and offers free tea and coffee and newspapers to MyWaitrose cardholders. These initiatives are about investing in the customers you already have so that they will recruit new ones for you. They, and dozens like them, have all been very successful, scoring very highly in the 'Measure the Magic' mystery shopper customer satisfaction surveys. In 2014, Waitrose won fourteen customer-service awards. Yet none of these initiatives, however well applauded, is enough to wow the customer on its own. The key to ensuring that the experience for all customers is excellent every time lies with each individual Partner. Even though tens of millions are invested in staff training and development every year, clearly flagging exactly how the customer experience should go, there are no guarantees Partners are going to do it every time.

Once again, employee engagement comes to the fore. Unengaged employees won't create engaged customers, however many hours you spend explaining how you'd like things done. Engaged employees will go above and beyond what is typically expected of them for the greater good of an organisation and its goals because they believe in the brand and are fully committed to upholding it. These people are innovators and ambassadors for your business, with the greatest potential to transform the customer experience in a positive way. They'll act as advocates too, with 78 per cent of engaged employees recommending their company's products or services, versus 13 per cent of the disengaged who'd give their employer the thumbs up.[35] When they are faced with the sort of obstacles that affect every business every working day, engaged employees are infinitely more likely to come up with solutions to overcome them. Higher levels of engagement strongly correlate to higher levels of innovation. Fifty-nine per cent of engaged employees say their job draws out their creativity, compared with just three per cent of disengaged employees.[36]

[35] Ipsos MORI.

[36] 'The Innovation Equation,' J. Krueger and E. Killham, *Gallup Management Journal*, 12 April 2007.

CASE STUDY

DPD is one of the UK's leading parcel delivery companies and employs more than five thousand people, operating more than three thousand vehicles from nearly fifty locations to deliver more than one million parcels a week. In 2011, the company introduced an ambitious employee engagement and customer-service training programme known as 'Be Amazing Every Day'. The programme, which saw more than four hundred training sessions for staff in the space of twelve weeks, encouraged the team to be proud of their personal performance and the brand. The individual talents and personalities of employees were featured on boards in every depot, and staff were given the opportunity to earn vouchers worth up to £20 as a thank you from managers for providing excellent customer service. The vouchers could be spent at high street shops and in attractions across the UK. Achievements were also celebrated on the DPD UK website.

The 'Be Amazing Every Day' programme saw:

- driver productivity increase from 70.7 to 75.5 stops per route

- driver retention after thirteen-week induction up from 65 per cent to 75 per cent
- employee satisfaction up by 5 per cent
- efficiency gains of £10 million.

Since then, DPD has won numerous awards for customer satisfaction, including being named as best delivery company in the UK by consumer champion Which? and winning the customer focus category at the National Business Awards.

As a business, your greatest opportunity lies in turning unengaged or merely 'satisfied' employees into engaged ones. The people who are closest to the customer know and understand much more about them than the management team at head office. They know the approach to take to give a company the competitive advantage. Your business will function at its best and your customers will be happiest if you put your employees' commitment, potential and creativity at its centre.

CHAPTER THREE

Taking responsibility

*You cannot have a long-term healthy business
without a healthy society*

---

*The Partnership aims to conduct all its business
relationships with integrity and courtesy, and
scrupulously to honour every business agreement.*

*The Partnership aims to obey the spirit as well as
the letter of the law and to contribute to the well-
being of the communities where it operates.*[37]

Spedan Lewis looked on responsibility as an active
requirement for both employees and the company.
If you own something you must take responsibility
for it and he wanted the Partnership to act as a 'good

---

[37] John Lewis Partnership: Our Principles

neighbour' and 'good citizen', always doing the right thing, long before Corporate Social Responsibility (CSR) was dreamed up. He realised that CSR isn't an initiative you do; rather it embraces everything you do and how you do it.

I have heard some people say that management is cheating shareholders if money is spent on CSR and that it is an indulgence of affluent societies and rich companies. The often-quoted free marketeer Milton Friedman believed executives should spend their own time and money on philanthropy, and let investors decide how to give away their money once profits had been distributed as dividends. It has even been argued that CSR is a distraction. I believe these views and actions have played a leading role in the increasing lack of trust in business and the growing discontent with capitalism I described at the beginning of this book. Acting responsibly is important to employees, customers and suppliers, and when aligned to your business strategy, as I'll set out later, boosts commercial returns.

In my view, damaging the planet and acting irresponsibly for the short-term benefit of those looking for a quick return on capital is morally bankrupt. What does it say about our responsibility as stewards of this world for future generations? It would not be hard to argue that capitalism has been disastrous for the environment. In Jewish tradition you leave the field fallow in the seventh year to recognise the fact that you do not own the land. And many religions struggle to understand why mankind is intent on harming what their god or gods created. As the biblical quote goes, 'For what does it profit a man to gain the whole world and forfeit his soul?' (Mark 8:36). Throughout history, religions, governments and philosophers have questioned why a minority is allowed to exploit the world's natural resources for its own financial ends.

Like many sectors, retailing is hugely competitive and perhaps even more so in recent years. You only have to look at the rise and rise of discount retailers to understand how price has taken centre stage in this intense rivalry. If one store group slashes the price of an item, it is not long before the next one does, and then the next one. You could be forgiven for concluding that they are all in a suicidal race to the bottom.

Milk is a case in point. When Asda cut the price of four pints from £1.53 to £1.25 in July 2010, it wasn't long before the major stores, including Waitrose, followed. Within months, so-called discount stores, such as Aldi and Lidl, upped the ante to sell the same quantity for just £1. This left Waitrose in a difficult position. At that time we were committed to paying our suppliers 73p for that quantity. Slashing prices and insisting suppliers take up the slack (as some competitors were doing) would be potentially catastrophic for our farmers. We decided to hold off from making any changes to see how the trend would affect volume.

It did. A lot.

Waitrose's milk sales went down 11 per cent in a month. We couldn't ignore the numbers and nor could our dairy farmers. We agreed on a strategy where we would reduce our price to match the market, but still continue to pay the same rate to the 60 or so dairy farmers who supplied our milk. In our view, our long-term commitment to them was more important than delivering an ultimatum that if they didn't share the hit, they were out.

This story is still playing out, with some retailers cutting the price of four pints of milk still further. The price shows some signs of stabilising, but there are now, more than ever, real question marks over the long-term sustainability of the UK dairy market. The low price received by some UK farmers, and the even lower amount being paid to some farmers in the Baltic states, means the balance of supply and demand is compounding the problems of an already volatile marketplace. Unsurprisingly, the number of UK dairy farmers has fallen to below ten thousand, compared with almost thirty-six thousand in 1995. The National Farmers Union has warned there could be fewer than five thousand dairy farmers left in the UK by 2025. Every day, farmers are being faced with a stark choice: cull cows, reduce production or leave the industry.

Why does this matter? Isn't it just globalisation and the free market at work? In my view it is a real concern. It represents the moral dilemma that is at the heart of society today. At a very basic level, the competitiveness of a company and the health of the communities around it are closely tied. A business needs a successful community to create demand for its products, to provide crucial assets and a supportive environment. A community needs successful businesses to provide jobs and opportunities to make money. People need to ask themselves what they value more: milk at under £1, or a thriving countryside, well maintained by farmers for all to enjoy. We are not self-contained entities. But sadly most consumers are unaware of these consequences – they just go for the cheapest option, oblivious to the wider consequences. Perhaps we should ask how we can educate consumers better so they can act with humanity.

Rightly or wrongly, business has earned a reputation as a major cause of social, environmental and economic problems. Detractors believe too many companies prosper at any cost, regardless of their impact on the broader community. From fraud to tax avoidance, to banking scandals and food contamination, there are plenty of headlines to fuel the idea that business is not always very responsible. For example, there was the horsemeat scandal, which saw a number of suppliers, including frozen-food-giant Findus, forced to admit that some of their ready-meal products contained

100 per cent horsemeat, rather than beef, as billed. Big-name clothing companies have also been in the spotlight following a spate of reports of appalling health-and-safety conditions in Third World factories, which have led to many worker deaths. In 2013, the Rana Plaza factory building in Bangladesh collapsed, killing more than 1,100 people and leading to calls for clothing brands to guarantee safe conditions for garment industry workers, even when those workers were paid by third-party suppliers. Yum Foods!, the owner of fast food giant KFC, has said it plans to stop sourcing packaging made from the resources of tropical rainforests following the furore over a former supplier, Asia Pulp and Paper, destroying Indonesian forests to source paper for KFC buckets. In 2011, a significant group of major fashion and footwear brands were compelled to address the issue of toxic chemicals used in the dyeing process and have committed to stop using them by 2020.

The big question is, how could we ever have thought any of these things were acceptable in the name of short-term financial rewards?

While the global financial crisis of 2008 became a focal point for discontent with the corporate world, in truth, dissatisfaction with the way we do business has been growing for years. And it is not a problem that is going to go away just because the economy is picking up. Global trust in the corporate sector has fallen to pre-financial-crisis levels. In 2015, trust in business fell in 16 of 27 countries surveyed, and in the UK, it fell from 56 per cent in 2014 to 52 per cent.[38]

The obvious question is, why is this a big issue now? Has the corporate world been a paragon of virtue for centuries only to have gone off the rails in the last decade or so? Perhaps a little, but nowhere near the extent reflected in the statistics. The growth in dissatisfaction is, in part, down to the digital revolution, which has transformed the dynamics of the relationship between business and society. Technology has not only changed the way we live, but also our social expectations of corporate transparency. In an age in which a company's environmental record and labour practices are readily

---

[38] '2015 Edelman Trust Barometer,' www.edelman.com.

available and can be tweeted and re-tweeted, like-minded people can easily find each other. People know how their food is produced, or how their iPhones are made and how we use the Earth's resources. Everything local is now global.

Another recent phenomenon is the perceived increased short-termism of many businesses today. Companies focused on short-term profitability are naturally reluctant to invest in CSR initiatives, which often only realise long-term benefits. While few would argue against the PR value of ploughing a percentage of profits into the community, or forgoing a proportion of profit to support hard-pressed suppliers, for some organisations and investors it falls into the bracket of 'nice to have'. The pressures for short-termism are intense, and its habits are deeply embedded in modern businesses. While investors and companies often say they accept the value of socially and environmentally responsible strategies, they still find it easy to ignore the broader influences that determine longer-term success.

Things will have to change, though. It doesn't matter how focused a company is on quarterly figures, it would be a short-sighted business indeed that chose to ignore how customers view it. Taking responsibility and doing the right thing has become the deciding factor in the brands people choose. Thus nine out of ten global consumers say they want the companies they buy from to go beyond the minimum standards required by law to operate responsibly and address social and environmental issues.[39] Of those surveyed, 87 per cent said they would consider boycotting companies that engage in irresponsible behaviour. More importantly, consumers are not just *more likely* to spend money with companies that do the right thing, but are also willing to pay any premium that goes with it. Another survey found that more than half (55 per cent) of global consumers are willing to pay extra for products or services from companies committed to positive social and environmental impact.[40] The numbers are on the rise too, up from 50 per cent in 2012 and 45

[39] 'Cone Communications/Echo Global CSR Study 2013,' conecomm. com.

[40] 'Corporate Social Responsibility Survey,' Nielsons, June 2014, www. nielsen.com.

per cent in 2011. Regionally, the figures are higher in Asia-Pacific (64 per cent), Latin America (63 per cent) and Middle East/Africa (63 per cent), increasing by 9, 13 and 10 percentage points, respectively, since 2011. However, interest in Europe is still strong (40 per cent), up 8 points since 2011, and don't forget, this is not just paying lip service to caring about the environment or poverty, this translates into real purchasing decisions. Once again, there is a real commercial imperative to listen to the market.

Behaving responsibly has an impact closer to home too. Giving employees a sense of pride about the difference they can make to their communities is an important component of empowerment and engagement. Employees are increasingly choosing to work for organisations whose values resonate with their own. Those who approve of their company's commitments to social responsibility have been found to be far more engaged and are more apt to believe that their employers are interested in their well-being. They also feel more favourably about the integrity of the senior people in their organisation and rate their company as more competitive.[41] There's a crucial role in staff retention too. It is no accident that 'commitment to CSR' has become a key criterion in the methodology used to compile 'Best Companies to Work For' lists. It is known to have a real impact on job satisfaction.

It's a huge draw for the next generation of employees too. Ask any student whether they believe it necessary to take into account the social and environmental impact of a business and the answer will invariably be a resounding yes. Three out of four of the Millennial Generation (born 1978–1998) want to work for a company that 'cares about how it impacts and contributes to society'.[42] They absolutely expect core values to be part of their working life.

The reality is, though, that while there are many ambitious, well-publicised strategies in this direction by many organisations, including major companies such as Unilever, Unipart and Kingfisher, we've still got a long way to go on meeting the expectations of

[41] Sirota Survey Intelligence, www.crmlearning.com.

[42] 'Past. Present. Future. The 25th Anniversary of Cause Marketing,' Cone Communications, Boston, MA, 2009, www.coneinc.com.

customers and society as a whole. Many of the changes made to working practices are small and incremental, even one-off corporate actions, rather than a complete change to the way business is done. There is an inescapable impression that some companies view social responsibility as a passing fad, something perhaps they can nod at without putting any real resources behind. Many corporate responsibility programmes that have emerged in reaction to external pressure are largely there to preserve a firm's reputation. At best they are dismissed internally as a necessary expense and at worst as an impediment to the day job. Behind it all is the hope that a few well-publicised, high-profile initiatives will do the job. They won't. Activities that generate limited, even one-sided benefits, such as one-off corporate donations, look one-sided. They may even backfire and be viewed as propaganda, or worse still, expose a company to criticism because it shows a gap between its words and actions. Employees, customers, suppliers and the wider community are looking for long-term, credible ideas that truly benefit society.

A strategy on responsibility should be incorporated

into the new approach to capitalism. Until now, while capitalism has been unparalleled for meeting human needs, improving efficiency, creating jobs and building wealth, we have fallen into the trap of taking too narrow a view. Our interpretation is preventing us from harnessing capitalism to meet society's broader challenges. This is not to say we want businesses to only be charitable donors. We don't. We need businesses to act like businesses in this respect as much as everything else because in this way they can be the most powerful force in addressing the issues we all face. In chapter eight I will describe how some companies have aligned their business strategy to be both responsible and drive commercial returns.

The purpose of any organisation should be to create long-term value, not just short-term profit. The goal is to create value through the assets a business has, through both its people and products, and then reinforce its values at every turn. Working responsibly will drive the next wave of innovation and productivity in the global economy.

Reconnecting companies and communities after

many years of being lost in short-term management will open up new and better ways to develop products, serve markets and build productive companies. This approach is the opportunity to reshape capitalism and its role in society. It is also the way to restore trust in business. None of this needs to raise costs. When you work for societal needs, not just conventional economic ones, the expense does not necessarily flow in just one direction. Well-thought-through initiatives mean firms can be more innovative through new technologies, operating methods and management approaches, which will in turn increase productivity and expand markets.

There are a considerable number of new social enterprises embodying this approach, as well as large existing businesses, such as B&Q now hiring power tools as well as selling them, or Marks and Spencer's 'Shwopping' initiative which gives vouchers to spend on new clothes when old ones are recycled through Oxfam. Waitrose has seen proof of the value of this sort of approach time and again. As the milk story at the beginning of this chapter illustrated, the business was repaid by the loyalty of suppliers and supported by customers. In another example, some Waitrose suppliers in South Africa have recently come under enormous pressure from lucrative offers from Chinese buyers who are taking great interest in the region as a food source for its growing population. A great deal of money has been put on the table but, while some farmers undoubtedly teetered, none have changed. The view was that many of them had been supported by Waitrose for twenty-five years and more, through good times and bad. The deals on offer today might look good, but what would they be next year and the year after that? There was no guarantee that these new buyers would display the loyalty and support of the Partnership.

As the Partnership repeatedly finds, success is founded on the passion of Partners who are always willing to step up. They are also encouraged to volunteer (75,000 paid hours are made available each year), building stronger links with local communities, enabling them to do 'something more' in their jobs to produce something of value to both business and society.

> ### CASE STUDY
>
> Unilever engaged its 170,000 employees *en masse* in its Sustainable Living Plan, launched in 2010. As a result, the consumer-goods giant reported greatly improved motivation and loyalty and said it was better placed to attract talent. The aim of Unilever's initiative is to improve the health of one billion people, buy 100 per cent of its agricultural raw materials from sustainable sources and reduce the environmental impact of everything it sells by one-half, while doubling its revenues. Recipes of food products have been reformulated to reduce trans-fat, saturated fats, sugar and salt, while many of the company brands, such as Dove, have been linked to social causes. The message behind the campaign changed the thinking that they were *selling* to customers, and instead *serving* their communities. The firm is working hand-in-hand with its team to address economic, social and environmental challenges.

Political powers and NGOs can't be expected to take up the slack while others get on with the serious business of making money. We are all, as they say, in this together, and this is why collaborative coalitions, such as Business in the Community, have been so successful. Business has a significant role to play. Society's needs are large and growing, and an entire generation needs business to step up. Many of the most successful CSR projects are collaborations between business and other organisations, whether it is charities, or political or community groups. Each group brings its own unique skills to the party and by working together collaborations can achieve so much more.

Take politics as an example. It is the role of the ruling political party to create the conditions for companies to be the most successful that they can be. It is the only way for an economy and a society to flourish. How else will the health service, defence, police and social services be paid for unless there is a thriving economy generating activity, with businesses paying corporation tax and other taxes and employing people who also pay tax? Yet be under no illusions. It is only the business sector that can make the economy strong, not the other way around. We need to work together.

The 2017 the current UK government is doing a great deal to fulfil its side of the contract. Corporation tax is low and being reduced further and regulations are being cut. In return, companies bear a responsibility to the communities they serve. This is not something business should fear. In fact, these pressing challenges offer a great opportunity to grow our corporate leadership, create meaningful sustainability strategies and engage better with society as a whole. When business fully engages in a social issue, the impact can be spectacular, actually saving the taxpayer money.

Take Timpsons, the shoe repair company, which has devised a training programme for prisoners while they serve their sentence and then offers them a guaranteed trial job on their release. How much cheaper is it for the taxpayer that these people find gainful employment than end up back in the criminal justice system? There are many other examples of creative collaborations, which enable things to happen that would not normally be possible. Forward-looking companies are using their corporate resources, from funding for staff skills, to offering products and services to support the communities in which they operate. A partnership between PA Consulting Group and Teach First, a UK charity that places graduates into schools in low-income areas to raise education standards, is typical of this approach. A number of employees, including Chief Executive Alan Middleton, went back into the classroom, harnessing their expertise and knowledge in a very different environment. It is a mutually beneficial experience. Other initiatives boost the bottom line while enhancing the world in which we live. Veolia, the water and waste utility company, derives 19 per cent of its revenue from products once considered to be waste, but that are now sold and reintroduced into the supply chain. Some of the advantages are more long-term. A partnership between Manchester Airport and Manchester Enterprise Academy to improve school performance is also intended to build a pipeline of skilled employees for the future. Waitrose recently arranged to inform people's next of kin if home delivery drivers became concerned when they called on elderly customers. It's a small, yet significant way of bringing reassurance and comfort.

The demand for companies to meet the needs of society is not going to go away. It will require a new way of thinking for many of us, but it will enable us to utilise our skills, resources, management capability and the talent of our teams to lead social progress. This is an opportunity for us all to become better, more innovative and more effective businesses. These transformations will drive progress and will give firms that truly connect with their stakeholders a real competitive advantage. In return, we will win their respect, trust and loyalty.

The first step is the happiness and engagement of the workforce. They want to do the right thing by the community they live in and in shaping the society they want. In short they want responsibility. In his Principle 1, Spedan Lewis said that Partners should 'share the responsibilities of ownership as well as its rewards'. This sentence, and the idea behind it, spawned a completely different governance structure in Spedan's Partnership.

It does seem ironic that, if acting on behalf of shareholders is the Holy Grail for executives, their trust is continually questioned by new legislation. While big scandals lead to substantive changes in corporate governance and reporting, such as the Cadbury Report or Sarbanes-Oxley, each year the Financial Standards Authority produces new best guidance. The aim: to improve transparency for shareholders. The implication to my mind is that management cannot, in fact, be trusted to act in their shareholders' best interests, despite their claims to be putting them first.

But what if all your shareholders work inside your business? What does that mean for risk and audit, remuneration or CSR board sub-committees? And what if you elect members from your shareholder workforce to sit on the board? Would external non-executive directors still be needed to check that shareholders' interests were paramount, or focus more on adding commercial value from their experience? What if the entire workforce were to take responsibility for their actions and the business as a whole, ever mindful of their impact?

This is a different approach, but hugely effective. One of the keys to employee engagement is empowerment through trust and responsibility, but it seems to run contrary to the current trend in business, which has established a costly system where the checkers check the checkers! Yet none of it seems to stop the scandals and recriminations. As a result, responsibility, when it comes to it, is quickly shifted at the tick of a box. If employees really cared about how their actions impacted on the business, customers, suppliers, communities and society, and were trusted to act in its and their best interests, that would be powerful, wouldn't it?

In the second part of this book I set out how Spedan Lewis turned his principle of a fairer workplace into practice.

Part two

In Practice:
Six Steps to Workplace Happiness

Chapter four

Step One: Reward and recognition

One size cannot engage all

Spedan Lewis wanted to share the rewards of owning the company with his fellow Partners. His aim was to reward their individual efforts through a pay system that acknowledged individual performance, collectively shared annual profits as a bonus based on a percentage of everyone's pay and, remarkably, allow employees to indulge their hobbies and passions in the way a successful business owner would. To this day the Partnership still has five ocean-going yachts, two golf courses, five country houses for Partners to stay in and every club and society imaginable with generous subsidies. In many companies that once had these types of benefit they have been sold or stopped to give the cash instead to the shareholders. Spedan, however, realised that reward went beyond a pay rate. He saw how his all-embracing approach to engagement built self-esteem. And to reward longevity of service and promote self-development twenty-six weeks paid leave is awarded after twenty-five years service.

It's worth reflecting for a moment longer on the cleverness of this idea: a pay rate commensurate with your individual contribution; a staff bonus at the same percentage rate for all, but calculated on your annual earnings, which reflects your contribution; and your personal interests and hobbies catered for and highly subsidised. How different that feels from a world where labour's share of GDP – the wealth generated by business – has decreased since the millennium, while the share to capital – those that provide the finance – has increased. Corporate profit margins are at their highest level since the Second World War and trillions of dollars sit on company balance sheets and in banks, on and off-shore, in corporate America alone. Imagine the impact on the economy if even a proportion of that were released to those who had helped to create that wealth.

However, reward has to be put into context.

Renowned business management psychologist Frederick Herzberg's theory of motivation in the workplace is that pay and working conditions can only ever minimise an employee's dissatisfaction with work. Neither pay nor working conditions are enough to promote satisfaction or engagement on their own merits. Employees are motivated by a range of other factors, but most notably responsibility, achievement, recognition, type of work and potential for advancement, all of which I'll discuss in later chapters. In other words, if you want fully engaged employees, and to reap all the commercial advantages that go with it, you can't just throw money at the issue. Achieving a fully engaged workforce runs a lot deeper than that. Reward and recognition is about acknowledging a job well done. To feel committed to an organisation, individuals have to take pride in doing their job. Become a business where people actively want to work and the workforce will willingly do more than is expected of them and go the extra mile. In turn, engaged employees will positively influence the behaviour of customers. Their excitement and enthusiasm rubs off on the people they serve.

Herzberg's theory has been backed by research that shows the drivers of engagement are linked to behaviour and approach, not simply pay and benefits.[43] This perhaps goes to show why many of the companies that consistently appear in 'Best Companies to Work For' lists are not necessarily the best payers. The main drivers of employee engagement were found to be:

- Leadership – People want leaders that are consistent, effective and who show a sincere interest in their teams.

- Stress – Employees quite rightly demand good management of work/life balance, with their employer getting staffing levels right and allowing them as much autonomy as their role allows.

- Goals – The goals of both business and individuals should be clearly and explicitly understood and expressed.

[43] '2012 Global Workforce Study,' Towers Watson.

- Managers – Line managers need to be consistent and willing to provide appropriate coaching.

- Company image – A good public image is important. Employee satisfaction is closely linked to their view of their employer and the feelings of the community at large.

None of this is to say we can ignore pay altogether. In fact, far from it. Pay is a key concern for everyone, and if you are not paying a fair salary no amount of recognition for a job well done will be enough to make your employees forget they are not being paid enough. Your pay scale has to meet expectations.

Pay should also absolutely reflect a worker's contribution to the business. Financial reward for discretionary effort is still a significant driver for employees around the globe. This is the reason the Partnership doesn't have a single point pay range. Cashiers at many rival chains receive a basic rate for the job, but this means that however hard an individual works, they will not be recognised for the value they are creating. The Partnership's pay ranges start with a training rate and then progress upwards by up to 30 per cent, with considerable premiums for those who develop as specialists. Line managers review each Partner's performance every year, assessing them on a range of measurements. They are awarded whatever pay increase is warranted for their performance in the previous twelve months. Some Partners will receive increases of 10 per cent, while others will get nothing at all. The overall wage bill may increase by, say, 2.5 per cent, but within that there will be a huge variation on what people are given based on how they have worked.

The message is clear: the better you perform, the better the money. And this drives commercial performance for the benefit of all. The pay policy, which is enshrined in the written Constitution, says the Partnership pays the market rate for the job and as much above as can be justified by performance. This means that performance management has to be robust and honest so that Partners can achieve their potential. It's impossible to duck a performance issue because it is reflected in each individual's annual pay review.

And the best managers are keen to coach and delegate responsibility to help those in their team achieve their maximum pay potential.

Of course, there is also the added incentive that each Partner feels a part-owner of the company, through a trust where the shares are held, which means they have a share in annual profits as well as an active say in how the business is run. But I should add that the amount of profit to be distributed is only calculated after sufficient funds are set aside for expansion and development. The long-term sustainability of the business must come first. Each generation is committed to hand the business on to the next in better shape. That means through good times and bad the senior executives and all levels in the company receive the same percentage bonus. You cannot have top executives collecting large bonuses even when the company is performing poorly. Everyone is in it together. Everyone is psychologically invested in the business and this engagement heightens productivity, profits and career satisfaction.

It is a structure that is beginning to be replicated elsewhere with a great deal of success among the hundred or so UK companies with significant employee ownership. Support is growing from a range of sectors too. In 2010, Lambeth Council announced plans to remould itself according to the 'John Lewis model' saying it would encourage community involvement in exchange for council tax rebates. The following year, David Cameron, at the time Prime Minister, talked at length about turning parts of the public sector into 'John Lewis-style' mutuals. There have been suggestions that state schools may prosper in this form and a number of NHS Trusts already operate along these lines. The Partnership has helped at least four to adapt to its way of doing business.

People from both the political and corporate worlds undoubtedly appreciate elements of what the Partnership does. They see the plaudits the Partnership gets and the long term consistent success of its stores and believe they'd like to be a part of that. Then they realise it means giving away the organisation to the employees and they have second thoughts.

For many, the principle of giving something away is hard to accept. Someone at the head of a family business who has worked hard for years would wrestle with passing it on to employees for no immediate financial gain. A business with thousands of shareholders would never vote to give it all to its workers. The theory sounds fine, but the practice appears too onerous.

Some have got around it by selling the business to the employees, or building up an employee trust fund over time, or finding ways to allow all employees to have shares in the business or share options, or paying a bonus to staff as part of the annual dividend. There are examples of national legislation too. In Mexico, state law says that businesses must share equally, amongst all employees, 10% of company profits. Perhaps that may contribute to Mexicans being the second most happy people on the planet! It can be done. It just needs a new way of thinking.

To make this model work you probably need to take a long-term view. Running a successful business is a marathon, not a sprint. If you invest in your people now, you will have a far, far stronger and more sustainable business in the future. You'll also have a more interesting one, with fully engaged employees who actively want to innovate and take things forward. Even if you are unable or unwilling to go all the way with an employee-ownership structure, there are elements of Partnership thinking that you can introduce today that will make a huge difference to your business. Adopt Partnership Lite and find a way to reward employees with shares or bonuses that reflect their contribution and you will immediately see raised levels of engagement and will reap the productivity benefits that go with it. If the company does well out of its workers' endeavours then they should be rewarded. If they then feel they have a genuine stake in the success they will be more committed.

One of the schemes that does this very effectively is run by fast food chain Pret A Manger, where founder Julian Metcalf's philosophy is that happy teams equal happy customers, which equals a happy business. The company's goal is to deliver top-notch customer service, aiming to serve consumers in an efficient and friendly manner within sixty seconds in a bright, quirky atmosphere. This strategy clearly relies on the personality and warmth of its staff. Each week, a mystery shopper visits every shop, looking for signs of excellent customer engagement. If the mystery shopper has a good experience, every member of the team in that branch gets an extra £1 per hour in their pay packet for the hours they worked in that week. Eighty per cent of branches get that bonus every week. I was so taken by the scheme I tried something similar in Waitrose, rewarding all members of a branch with a small and equal cash bonus if they achieved a certain performance target. It worked!

In my view if you run any sort of staff bonus scheme it should be run on an equitable basis like this. In the Partnership, each Partner is guaranteed an equal share in the benefits and profits of a business that puts them first. This is not a profit share scheme that is skewed towards senior management. All staff, from the chairman down to shelf-stackers, receive the same percentage annual bonus. Similarly, as set out in the constitution, the highest-paid director is not allowed to earn more than seventy-five times as much as a non-management employee. This may sound like a big difference, and it is, but then compare it to pay differentials at Britain's largest public companies. Oxfam's 2015 report on global inequality points out that in the world of FTSE 100 companies the typical CEO earns 183 times more than the average. And often the average is many times higher than the lowest levels. At the very top of the scale some are earning 810 times more.

I can never understand why shareholders believe that all that needs to be done rewards-wise is give large incentives to senior management. There is only ever so much senior staff can do. Yes, a good charismatic leader can move the dial, but beyond that, every organisation is reliant on individuals throughout the company to make it succeed. Pay and rewards need to be fair and equitable (and understood to be so at all levels) to be effective. As the table of priorities at the beginning of the chapter shows, trust in leadership is important and any perception of injustice within an organisation will have an impact on employee engagement. Employees need to know you are truly in it together and the division of bonuses is not just about fiscal gain, it is symbolic of how a business views the team. Get it right and it can have a powerful effect on engagement.

To show just how powerful this can be, I'll go back in time to relate a story from when I was retail director of Waitrose's stores in 2004. We'd bought a tranche of shops from Somerfield and spent around £2 million on refurbishing each one. The bill was quite high because we didn't believe in just giving a store a lick of paint and making sure all the customer-facing areas look the part. Once we'd taken over the stores, we made all the Somerfield team Partners and were therefore beholden to give them the same benefits as those in the rest of the business. Thus the staff dining rooms were revamped, as well as the toilets and so on. Shortly before the grand opening of one branch, someone left some rather unpleasant graffiti in the Partner male toilets. A local decorator was swiftly engaged by the branch manager who painted over the offending artwork at a cost of £200.

The following day, a note was left on each table in the staff dining area saying something to the effect of: 'We've spent £200 on a decorator to paint over graffiti in the toilets, which means £200 less in the bonus kitty.' All that sort of petty nonsense ended overnight. Everyone got the subtext to the note – harm the business and you are only harming your own prospects. When you treat people as stakeholders they take on a level of responsibility that you don't see anywhere else.

There is one further twist from that branch which supports my point. A week or so after the reopening, a cashier told the manager a colleague who had phoned in sick had really gone to see her sister. As the store was now her business she felt the action to be reprehensible. When the 'poorly' Partner returned to work, the manager spoke quietly to her, word got around, and absence in the branch fell from nine per cent pre our acquisition to under three per cent.

But what encourages this loyal action to become permanent? How do you police a large-scale organisation to make sure those that manage and are managed are living by its values?

There is a legal requirement for companies to have a 'whistle blowing' system but, as in so many ways, Spedan Lewis was well ahead of his time. He introduced a number of 'critical' management posts to ensure the executive was living by the Partnership's written constitution, which set out the company's aims and values. These posts were given glorious nineteenth-century titles, like 'General Inspector', 'Partners' Counsellor' and 'Chief Registrar', and they reported directly to the Chairman and Partnership Board. The General Inspector had the freedom to look into any area of the business he wished. The Partners' Counsellor was there to act as an ombudsman for Partners, hearing complaints and concerns, while the Chief Registrar was responsible for the efficiency and vitality of the Partnerships' democracy. They all gathered information and received feedback through a series of officers at local level, all independent of management. Some meetings were held without management present, so non-management Partners could express their views freely and anonymously. The minutes of meetings were openly displayed on staff notice boards, as were the minutes of more formal meetings where managers accounted to elected representatives for their actions and performance in their area of responsibility. Through this system of councils, committees and critical management, all Partners' views were heard and the direct access to the Chairman and board created a sense of belonging. And, as I will explain in the next chapter, sharing information and empowering employees further reinforces the right behaviours.

According to Maslow's hierarchy of needs, two of the most valuable psychological needs we have are the desire to be appreciated and to 'belong'. In other words, recognition is crucial. 'High recognition' companies have 31 per cent lower voluntary turnover than companies with a poor recognition culture.[44] Saying thank you and recognising a job well done goes a long way. Researchers have proved that when you thank someone, it releases oxytocin, a hormone that makes us more relaxed, collaborative and happy.[45]

[44] 'New Bersin & Associates Research Shows Organisations that Excel at Employee Recognition Are 12 Times More Likely to Generate Strong Business Results,' Bersin by Deloitte, 7 November 2012, www.bersin.com/News.

[45] 'How the Trust Hormone Drives Business Performance,' Josh Bersin, Forbes, 30 April 2012, www.forbes.com.

Case Study

Staff at construction and development firm Lindum Group own 45 per cent of shares in the Lincoln-based company. Every year, 10 per cent of profits are split among employees. Financial support is also offered towards training and qualifications, with 60 per cent of the team benefiting from this initiative.

Extra-curricular activities on offer include annual golf and cricket days, five-a-side football, bowling nights, family cycle rides and a subsidised gym. Recognition can be as simple as stopping work at 3pm on 4 July to celebrate Employee Ownership Day with an ice cream.

Lindum, which was one of the *Sunday Times* top 100 best companies to work for in 2013, employs 486 people, but only experienced forty sick days in the year to September 2014.

Reward and recognition strategies need to be ingrained in a company's DNA to drive discretionary effort and inspire a team to do more. It is no coincidence that 70 per cent of the *Sunday Times*'s top 100 employers invest in reward and recognition programmes. People want to work for employers who appreciate their endeavours. Values-based recognition programmes (which reinforce a company's culture and core values) positively impact on employee engagement by 90 per cent and enhance retention by 68 per cent.[46]

As well as structured reward and recognition programmes, I am a fan of encouraging spontaneous awards for staff who do more than is asked. I call them 'random acts of kindness' (the approach was used for customers too). We introduced the 'one step beyond' scheme, where managers are given a cheque book so they can instantly write out a reward, say a dinner for a staff member and their partner, for a job well done. We trusted managers to make their own decisions so no upward authority is needed. If a manager prefers they can hand out wine, flowers or chocolates – whatever they think is right. The aim is straightforward, to show that you care and have noticed someone's contribution on an ongoing basis, not just once a year at pay review time.

[46] '2015 Employee Recognition Report,' SHRM/Globoforce Survey, 22 June 2015.

Well thought-out reward and recognition initiatives, coupled with a conducive working environment, help create sustainable, long-term businesses that are beneficial to employees, the community and society as a whole. It all begins with employees, and making sure they are well looked after in all respects.

CHAPTER FIVE

Step Two: Information sharing

*The most important, yet most challenging,
element to full engagement*

I had a well-worn routine every Saturday night when I was leading Waitrose. I would sit down in a comfy armchair at home and ring around a number of branches. There was a core of three stores that I called every week, and then I randomly chose a different three. Almost every time the branch manager would talk in terms of 'we', as in:

'We are up by six per cent.'

Or:

'We have had a tough week.'

Every so often, though, there would be a manager who said 'I'. A clear warning we were going to have a problem at that branch.

The Partnership model is only ever as strong as the

people within it. This is the reason very careful attention is paid to the recruitment and training of the team. Not everyone will thrive in the Partnership environment, particularly if they have worked elsewhere at an organisation with an entirely different top-down approach. Those who prefer a 'them and us' traditional management structure struggle with regarding all work colleagues as equal owners. In particular, they are uncomfortable with the concept of sharing both data and ideas up, down and across the organisation.

To be fair, open discussion of performance does appear to be an unusual approach. Many, if not most, companies seldom share any substantive data with anyone other than the top tier of executives. And although there may be good reasons for so doing, for instance legal and commercial in publicly quoted companies, the subtext for some managers and the interpretation by many employees is very clear:

We'll tell you anything on a need-to-know basis and you don't need to know the rest.

In other words, employees are not an important part of the business. There must surely be no attitude more likely to erode engagement and commitment than this.

This closed-door approach doesn't just have a negative impact on engagement, it can directly impact on decision-making and therefore profitability. If workers don't see critical data on the place where they work, they won't know critical facts. They won't have a clue whether their division is healthy or in trouble. Nor will they have any handle on whether cash is abundant in the company, or whether there need to be cut backs that will affect everyone in the long term. They'll miss out on important detail on how the business is faring against the competition. At worst they will think their managers are manipulating the message to drive a particular action, and conspiracy theories begin, energy is wasted and trust is lost.

We all need to have a realistic and well-sourced view of the organisations where we work, regardless of whether we are the chief executive or work on the shop floor. The level of detail in which we receive it may be different, but information forms the basis of the decisions we make every day. Without it, we could all be heading off in completely the wrong direction. Maintenance may cut corners and trim back specification on essential new kit because they mistakenly believe the company is in a worse financial position than it actually is, or vice versa. Salesmen may agree to hefty discounts to shift stock, just at a time when a firm needs to keep margins steady. Product developers may relentlessly propose adding on all sorts of high-end additions when budgets are already stretched to the limits.

Committing to a culture that is open and transparent is central to employee engagement. 'An understanding of the bigger picture and a willingness to go beyond the requirements of the job' is one of the top five influences on employee engagement.[47] The other key factors are:

- A positive attitude towards and pride in the organisation

- A belief in the organisation's products/services

[47] 'The Drivers of Employee Engagement,' D. Robinson, S. Perryman, S. Hayday, Report 408, Institute for Employment Studies, March 2004.

- A perception that the organisation enables the employee to perform well

- A willingness to behave altruistically and be a good team player

A culture where information is freely given plays a role in each one of these key measures. Information is the basis of democratic participation. If you are a business that wants to get the best out of individuals on the team, openness is key. It is impossible to give people a greater say, or to demonstrate they have a share in the commercial success of your organisation, without equipping them with the full facts. You need to share with them as much knowledge as you are able, in order to give them the context for what you are trying to achieve. This doesn't mean a bunch of missives that come down from Head Office saying: this is our strategy. No; employees at all levels need a genuine overview of what is going on in their area and elsewhere. If employees understand the business, its strategy, how it is doing and who are the customers and competitors, they will make it stronger. Knowledge will unlock an influential role in important decisions. Individuals on the team will have valuable input on working methods and work together to coordinate their efforts.

The idea that knowledge should be freely shared is at the core of the Partnership philosophy and there are a number of ways to get the story out into the business. One of the things we introduced during my last year at Waitrose was the sharing of summarised Board minutes throughout the business. The aim is for complete openness, tolerance and freedom of expression at all times, as well as full opportunity for enquiry, criticism and suggestion. The ideal is maintained, even when there is a risk of controversy between Partners or outside the Partnership.

Thus in-house magazines are freely distributed, and Partners can write in anonymously. The letter and a reply from senior management are published within three weeks of receipt. They are a constant reminder that the Partnership is for all and no individual is beyond public scrutiny. Everyone is working for the common good. Knowledge-sharing is also facilitated through representative bodies with elected members, including branch forums and Partnership-wide councils. The Partnership's councils are key in enumerating Partners' concerns. These form lines of communication between Partners and council representatives and the Partnership Board and the Chairman. Information flows up and down the line and Partners are given a voice at every level and each part of the Partnership.

When Partners find a better way to do something, or feel they've dealt with an issue well, they are encouraged to share the news with the rest of the business. They can do so via the 'Good Suggestion Scheme' or through the group meetings managers have each month. Partners are also encouraged to spend time at other branches as part of the continuous improvement programme.

By taking responsibility for decision-making and information-sharing, the business delivers more. Employees understand the 'why' behind their jobs, 'what' they are expected to achieve and 'how' it is important to the greater good of the organisation.

> ### Case Study
> Bolton-based Asons Solicitors gives each of its 260-strong workforce daily updates on individual and group successes. The personal injury firm has seen its head count double every two years, thanks in part to its family-firm mentality that supports employee engagement and development. Staff have spoken out to say they have confidence in the leadership skills of managers and that the open and honest culture helps them fulfil their potential.

None of this means that those at the top have *less* information or knowledge, simply that overall the business becomes flatter and information is spread throughout the organisation. It makes for effective decision-making and involvement at all levels. But it requires managers to behave differently: accept and welcome challenge, be collaborative and thoughtful, explain actions and embrace good ideas, no matter where they come from.

All companies get narrow at the top. It doesn't matter how intelligent the senior executives are, or how effective their teamwork is, we've all got limitations to our problem-solving capacity or ability to respond quickly. In quick-fire trading businesses in particular, there are too many demands on management time, too many decisions to be made and stakeholders to satisfy. It makes sense, therefore, to involve employees, providing them with a full picture of business strategy, processes, quality, feedback and results. They are then better able to meet customers' expectations in the way senior managers might in their shoes. In Waitrose, all customer concerns are passed back to the branch involved to resolve rather than being handled through a remote, supposedly more efficient, centralised call centre. The constant feedback and trust that the branch Partners will do the right thing keeps engagement and service standards high and improving. Branch Partners feel the full responsibility for their actions and as a result, act on this, so the company immediately becomes more efficient. Collaboration is valued and teams communicate to get projects done because it directly affects them and their enjoyment at work. Consequently, leaders listen to employee feedback and encourage it.

Putting people first isn't for everyone. It might sound risky focusing all your energy inside the company, rather than on the customer or shareholders. One of the most common responses to the idea of sharing information is: we are a publicly traded company, we are not allowed to freely share data internally, otherwise we will have to make it publicly available for transparency's sake and this will create volatility in our share price. This sentiment, to avoid short-termism, is admirable from an external perspective, but makes employees feel as though they are operating in the dark. From the outset, Spedan Lewis shared weekly sales figures for the company and all business units with all Partners, creating a real sense of accountability in all areas. They are as a consequence publicly available each week. Sir Charles Dunstone, the talented and charismatic founder of Carphone Warehouse, once told me this openness was one of the elements of the Partnership's arrangements he would most like to replicate, but his advisers had warned against the move. It's worth thinking for a moment what percentage of your company's effort goes into informing shareholders on performance as opposed to employees.

It must also be worth thinking through what can be said to employees to explain how their company is doing, without breaching the ever-stricter confines of Stock Exchange rules. Thus, there is nothing to say that you can't share data with individual business units and departments. This sort of information is never made public anyhow. People sometimes say to me that they would be worried that commercially sensitive information could be leaked to competitors, which is true. But I have always felt the benefits of having an informed and engaged workforce far outweigh the downside. Plus, in my experience, these fears are unwarranted. Firstly because competitors spend most of their time thinking of reasons to rubbish their other competitors' plans. And secondly because if they did decide to follow they would need to change their own strategy and would then be just a pale imitator. It is also a question of trust. There is little point saying you put your staff first if you blatantly don't. If you trust individuals with sensitive information, or sharing data becomes an accepted part of your company culture, it is rare to find someone who betrays that trust. If you trust your team they will reward you with their engagement and loyalty. Trust takes time to build and you need to work at it. It certainly isn't a short-term strategy.

Once you've bought into the idea of sharing information, the obvious questions are: who gets to see it and how much do you tell them? Companies are often inclined to reserve the bulk of financial data for top levels of management. The train of thought is that those in the 'lower orders' either won't understand complex figures, or won't be interested, or both. Again, nothing could be further from the truth. Yes, not everyone is keen on statistics, but a surprising number of people are, particularly if the statistics are presented in a palatable way and even more so if their bonuses are based on profitability.

As well as weekly meetings to discuss sales and key performance targets, it is common in Waitrose to see the numbers posted in staff areas, even on a daily basis. Where there might be real concern about a precise number, ratios are used to make a case and help understanding. If your mindset is to engage by sharing, there is always a way.

In the next chapter we will look at how individuals might use that information to make a company stronger. In an environment where the ideal for any company must surely be for each employee to think and act like a CEO, so they can make smart decisions, helping them to be fully informed has to be one of the smartest decisions of them all.

Chapter six

Step Three: Empowerment

Turning all employees into engaged players

My family home is in a small north Dorset town with a very close-knit community. One of my neighbours is a former City Link delivery driver. City Link famously collapsed into administration on Boxing Day 2014, putting three thousand workers out of a job, including a thousand self-employed van drivers and agency workers. My neighbour had actually been made redundant six months earlier when our local depot closed, no doubt as the company struggled to square its troubled business. Luckily he managed to secure a pay-off and he used it to set himself up in business as a freelance delivery driver.

When we met up one day, I asked him: 'So, what is the difference between owning your business and working for City Link?'

He thought about it for a moment and then said with a grin: 'Huge.'

I pressed him to explain.

'Well, when I worked for City Link, I did my hours and went home. Now, if I get a phone call asking me to deliver a parcel, I do it. It doesn't matter what time it is, day or night.

'With City Link, I didn't care about my van at all. To be honest, I trashed the thing. I drove it as fast as I could because I knew if it went wrong I could get a new one. Now I have my own van I drive at a sensible speed and check it over every Friday: oil, water, tyres, everything. I really look after it. I know if I can make it last two years by caring for it, I'll make more money.

'The other thing is, I had an awful uniform at City Link. I hated it. I wear a shirt and a tie every day now and it looks great. Customers think I look really sharp when they sign for their parcels. I'm certainly getting a lot of local referrals.

'I make a lot more money now things have changed.'

This is a really good example of what a difference it makes if someone feels they own something – they care more. This man is motivated by getting a share of the rewards, he has the information he needs to do his job properly and a degree of power and influence. The fact he is instrumental in making his own life better is reflected in how hard he works.

The aim of any business must surely be to make their employees feel like this and this means making them a key part of the decision-making process, listening to their ideas and integrating their suggestions into your strategy.

There is a significant incentive to do so: teams that are inclusive outperform their peers by an impressive 80 per cent. In one study, one of the highest-rated issues in employee engagement was their organisation's willingness to 'listen to an employee's perspective'.[48] Reward your team by giving them freedom, power, trust, autonomy and encouragement and they will be more productive because they feel more in control. Allowing employees to make decisions on their own, and letting them experience the success that follows,

[48] '2014 Employee Recognition Trends Report,' Quantum Workplace.

helps them feel valued and rewarded. They associate success with their own abilities, which in turn motivates them to strive for more in future tasks.

By keeping your team informed and empowering them to use their knowledge, individuals will add value by:

- doing more complicated tasks

- being better at managing and controlling themselves

- coordinating their work with other employees

- suggesting ideas about better ways to work

- developing new products and ways to serve customers.

Engaged employees boost productivity because they direct their energy towards the right tasks and outcomes. The only way this can happen is if you give them the knowledge and equipment to do so and the confidence to use their own judgement.

This is a very different approach from the one you find in a hierarchical organisation, where individuals in the 'lower ranks' follow carefully laid out, routine, low-value tasks in a fairly controlled environment, leaving senior management to think the big thoughts, make decisions on strategy and coordinate between the various functions. As I set out in the previous chapter, the prerequisites for empowerment are sharing information and encouraging feedback. This develops individuals and helps them to operate more effectively, which benefits the company as a whole. When a company is ruled by top-down management, no one ever asks anything of people who probably know many of, if not all, the answers. One of the beauties of the John Lewis Partnership is that it has mobilised ninety thousand people to make the business better in every way.

Returning to the issue of customer service, first outlined in chapter two, empowering Partners to take the initiative and resolve customer complaints is what drives the Partnership's success in this area. Authority to do this has been devolved to the lowest level. Partners know that if someone comes in to their shop and something is not right, it is within their remit to put it right. How they choose to resolve the issue is up to them.

Many organisations are very prescriptive about the way complaints are dealt with. Some even have a set of rules pasted up on the wall behind the cash tills that is headed by the statement 'Refunds Policy', which an employee can point at without using any judgement! On the contrary, in Waitrose teams are expected to use their judgement. It is, after all, not the management facing the shopper, who may be furious about something that seems to have gone wrong. The Partner is in the best position to decide upon the best course of action. It is their business and these are their customers. If they want to see them again, they'll make the right call. They are trusted to make sensible decisions and they invariably do. And, as I explained in the chapter on customer service, loyal customers are the most profitable.

Similarly, the opening hours of each Waitrose shop is not dictated. There's a framework, where they may open from 8am to 8pm, but it is up to individual branches to decide if that is right for their area. It may be that a particular store is bang in the centre of commuter country and many customers do not arrive back into the area until late. The branch may decide to open longer in the evenings to capture this trade. The judgement call is theirs, which is so much more engaging and stops any notion of a them versus us culture. It's better for profits too.

The sharing of power is enshrined in the Partnership's constitution. Partners are invited to vote on key decisions and elect representatives to both the Partnership Council (a representative body like the British Parliament) and the Board. The use of the vote in the Partnership is a mechanism for ensuring that management is accountable to the workforce. Managers are free to manage, but at the same time need to do so according to the interests of the co-owners and with full accountability to the managed. To actively encourage a two-way dialogue, there is a wide range of initiatives in place so that every Partner that wants to can have a say in the way the business is run, right down to the fact that every single Partner is free to walk up and ask any director or senior manager a direct question about the business, or make a suggestion. This is not a chore for management. In fact, it is a source of invaluable insight. The notion that workers can't possibly have anything of use to contribute belongs firmly in the last century.

Partners are asked every day: How can you do your job better? How can you be more effective? What would you change to make the business better? If you are asked properly, and if you care, you will answer honestly.

There is no reason why this can't work effectively elsewhere, regardless of the ownership structure. In fact, it could change things overnight. Say, for example, all the nurses and doctors in an NHS Trust were gathered together and told: 'We have a way to make this better'. They would undoubtedly listen. Imagine they were all offered a share of the working benefits, but it was explained to them that to do this their organisation would need to be very open about the financial circumstances and the pressures the Trust was under to deliver. When they understood, every one on the team would then be empowered to make decisions to help save money and improve the service. People would say: we can find a cheaper way of ordering. Or, we can find a better way of covering hours. Or we can find savings here or there. Engaging employees and entrusting them with the information they need will give them all the incentive and power they require to transform their organisation. I saw countless examples of this every day in Waitrose. Partners came up with a remarkable range of suggestions from 'big picture' ideas on company direction and continuous improvement, to thoughts on how to improve daily life at work. Even seemingly insignificant proposals can make a tangible difference, like a set place for scissors or brooms in stockrooms, which saves time and cost. It leads to the view that 100 x 1% improvements are better than 1 x 100% improvement, that evolution through empowerment drives commercial success.

I think it worth exploring the psychology behind this seemingly banal scissors example for a few moments as it demonstrates the real power behind employee engagement. Most junior managers would understand and embrace the concept of 'right equipment, right place, right time' to improve efficiency. They might, therefore, instruct a board to be made and fixed in the stockroom on which scissors could be hung and to which they were returned after use. This would save time when looking for scissors to unwrap stock. It might also reduce the number of scissors being 'lost' and expensively reordered. Whilst undoubtedly some members of staff would welcome the improved organisation, many would see new 'rules', less freedom, and a company's relentless drive for efficiency. If, on the other hand, non-management staff are encouraged to come up with ideas to make their working lives easier and better and the company more profit, which they will share in, and they are empowered to put those ideas in place, the psychology is very different. Employees have control over their daily lives, they can be rewarded for making the business better and take pride in *their* achievements. It's an approach where management facilitate, encourage, inform, coach and reward rather than direct, control and enforce.

Years of creating this sort of culture at Waitrose means that Partners take responsibility as a matter of course. For instance, if a cage of goods arrives at a Waitrose store damaged, rest assured someone will query the way it has been packaged and delivered further back in the process. They won't dismiss it with a shrug and get on with something else, which is something that frequently happens in other businesses. They immediately recognise that this problem may well have a long-term impact on the financial outlook and the success of the company. They take responsibility for the issue. Similarly, all Waitrose delivery drivers carry spare sets of keys to open warehouse gates. This is something drivers elsewhere are often not prepared or trusted to do, meaning that an additional member of staff has to be available for this task. But the Waitrose drivers understand the cost saving and efficiency benefit and are prepared to go the extra mile – excuse the pun – and it makes a world of difference. Add together all these apparently incidental small changes and it is easy to see how they can have a noticeable effect on the success of a business.

We are all motivated by autonomy, mastery and purpose. We all want to leave our unique fingerprint on something good. It's great to say: 'I did that.' It is very rare for anyone to abuse this power. In fact, empowered employees take huge pride in making the right decisions.

I saw some fantastic examples of this following the set-up of the Waitrose Foundation in various locations in Africa. Employee councils were established at each of the farms we sourced from, and Waitrose and our exporters allocated funds based on the volume of their produce customers bought. It was up to the councils to decide exactly what they wanted to spend their money on. A passionate debate ensued. In one community, they decided to buy bicycles because many workers had a twenty-mile round trip to and from their place of work. In another, they invested in developing an off-shoot crafts business because the seasonality of fruit-picking meant paying work was only available for a maximum of two months a year. By transferring their skills to produce shoes and jewellery, the community was able to make money all year round. Plus, we were able to work with John Lewis to find sales outlets for these new products. Many other communities decided to invest in education for their children and in building basic facilities, such as toilet blocks and crèches. They could have decided to distribute the cash selfishly, but each group thought creatively about what they could do to make their community better. It was both humbling and inspiring, and infinitely better than the management deciding what they thought best!

When John Spedan Lewis first envisaged the Partnership model, he didn't think for one moment sharing power was the 'easy' option. Indeed he specifically raised the point that conflict between management and workers was natural, but his view was that democratic processes and broad engagement would be enough to resolve conflicts. What I found in my time at the Partnership was that managers and team leaders needed a practical framework of meetings, systems and support to manage the relationships within the team and to create the environment where Partners felt engaged and able to make the best decisions. The most effective way to do this was to help Partners to do the following.

- Feel valued – If individuals feel appreciated and listened to, as well as appropriately rewarded, they will give more of themselves.

- Freely voice ideas – We are always very receptive

to new ideas and prepared to engage in a two-way debate. This culture encourages Partners to talk freely about a wide range of topics, even difficult ones.

- Reject conflict – Regular, good-quality feedback is accepted as an important part of improving performance levels and it is quickly acknowledged that everyone is working to the same end but brings different experiences and view points. Conflict is, therefore, minimised and time is not wasted.

- Work as a team – When it is well known that all abilities are recognised and encouraged, Partners have positive feelings about the job and their colleagues. There is a drive to achieve on a personal level as well as to support each other.

- Manage differences – An atmosphere of collaboration ensures that differences are not allowed to get in the way, or to become a simmering source of conflict. In fact, differing views are seen as a strength.

- Take ownership – By creating a no-blame environment where people are encouraged to talk openly, rather than moan about things behind closed doors, Partners are more willing to take joint responsibility with management.

But none of this means that leadership is not necessary under a Partnership structure.

CASE STUDY

St Luke's was one of the brightest stars in the advertising world in the 1990s, attracting major-league clients, such as BT, the government and BSkyB. It created famous campaigns, such as 'Chuck Out the Chintz' for furniture giant IKEA and was named agency of the year in Britain in 1996, in just its second year in business.

Founders Andy Law, Kate Stanners and David Abraham created the business as a cooperative, with every member of staff given a share in the business

---

and a say in how it was managed. Much was made of its innovative approach: it was one of the first companies to introduce hot desking where employees (or co-owners) had no fixed workspace. There were no job descriptions and everyone on the team was encouraged to work outside their usual remit. Staff could also pursue other interests, such as film-making or music, as part of their working day and were entitled to a four-week sabbatical every five years as well as being given fifty hours off each year for social projects. Potential work could be (and was frequently) turned down on ethical grounds. Staff were kept fully informed on anything relating to the business as a whole, from major investments to new products, services or technology.

While the creativity at St Luke's was exceptional, the concept was not ultimately successful under this structure. Staff felt uncomfortable with some elements of the cooperative. A Channel 4 fly-on-the-wall documentary showed internal politics still dogged this seemingly most democratic of organisations, with staff rowing about the ethics of sending each other flowers to reward hard work. Many elements introduced to create a more open structure rankled. For example, workers were invited to set their own pay, which was then to be publicised. While Andy Law did so, no one else was keen to follow the lead.

This story illustrates how challenging democracy can be. There was nothing wrong with the idea of St Luke's; indeed it was a creative and inspiring project and was undoubtedly hugely successful in its heyday under that structure (the company thrives today under a different guise). What could perhaps have been better was its execution. While it is crucial that Partners, or co-owners, are given information and the power in which to express their views, it all needs to have controls and be properly managed. Everyone should have their say, but management is the ultimate decision-making power and will be held to account for the choices and direction they choose to take. Strong leadership is crucial.

This is not an unfamiliar structure for anyone. It's pretty much in parallel with the way we run and manage the United Kingdom. We have a cabinet made up of MPs from the leading political party, which makes decisions and is held accountable by Parliament and every five years by the electorate. This is similar to the Partnership's system of councils at local and national level all holding the various tiers of management to account. And, as explained earlier, it has a 'critical function', independent of management, and is there to provide a loyal opposition and ensure the management are working to Partners' best interests and in accordance with policy and the constitution. The government's actions are also chronicled and scrutinised through the media, just as they are through John Lewis and Waitrose in-house magazines, where anonymous letters are published and respectfully answered. Ultimately, though, the cabinet has the final say, just as the Executive Boards in the Partnership do.

It can be challenging, but you can only ever prosper with the support of your 'public'. It is one thing being told once that a decision is not well received and another being told again and again. Thanks to the structure, Partners are encouraged to make their feelings known, and do so particularly when they feel something is unfair. The success of the Partnership is down to people caring more and management listening and acting.

Devolving power will feel strange to many managers. There will be a reluctance to ask workers what they need to make their life better for fear the answer will be very self serving, or it will be a blunt request for more money. It is, however, very rare for this to happen. In the vast majority of cases, individuals will come back with fantastic ideas about how they can make their role more efficient, which will in turn make the company more profitable. They will have the answers. If in doubt, try this straightforward experiment. In a review, ask the individual what you can do to make their life at work better and more enjoyable. I will wager that nine times out of ten they will suggest something which will make the business better.

Leaders who try to enforce and police everything stifle collaboration. Setting out best practice and guidelines is fine, but it's just as important to give employees the tools and let them get on with what they need to do. In this approach leaders are coaches and skilled communicators. They focus on creating a culture for people to give their best. Leaders are still accountable, but through serving their teams, rather than the other way around.

My inescapable conclusion is that if action and reaction are best delivered at a local level to maximise engagement and increase customer satisfaction, then a decentralised, devolved corporate organisation works best, no matter how seemingly inefficient at times. For if those making decisions are removed from the effects they have created, particularly in a customer business, that dislocation will lead to resentment, distrust and the very lack of efficiency centralisation was aiming to bring. More often than not those working in the corporate centre are inclined towards building a bigger, more controlling edifice and thirst for more knowledge, rather than pushing in the opposite direction of driving engagement through trust and responsibility.

Chapter seven

Step Four: Well-being

As ye sow, so shall ye reap

Long before the National Health Service was established, Spedan Lewis was providing health services and social housing for his employees. Writing to his wife in 1929, he set out that 'health should come first, income should come next and happiness should come last of all'. He reasoned that the first two were prerequisites to the latter and to the business's success. As I will explain, Spedan's view on health went much further than physical well-being, to include early, and for the time radical, thinking about sustaining mental health.

Companies looking to improve their performance follow a well-worn route. They'll invest in technology and innovation, or provide better training for their workers, or perhaps find ways to cut back on waste.

Or maybe all of the above. While each of these actions can make a real difference, there is something closer to home that can have an even greater impact: looking after the health and well-being of your team.

Let me illustrate this with a true story. When George Warburton ran his family bread company one of his young drivers had a terrible accident, damaging his legs and back when away from work. George made sure the young man's job was kept open for a year. You might think that remarkable enough, but he went even further with an act of caring that demonstrated to everyone in the business how much he valued them. He arranged for the injured driver to have three hours of physiotherapy a week with the medical team at Bolton Wanderers Football Club, where he was a director. Each week, George would pick up the chap from his terraced home, drive him to the football ground, wait for him while he was being treated and then deliver him back home. The young man, then twenty-one years old, was so grateful he worked for Warburton's all his career and rose to be a senior manager. He couldn't have been more committed. As Theodore Roosevelt once observed, 'No one cares how much you know, until they know how much you care!'

It's surprising how little some companies do to invest in their team's well-being. It's even more shocking when you look at it in contrast to the norm in professional sport, where individuals are constantly looked after by teams of psychiatrists, physiotherapists, individual trainers and dietitians, and receive advice on investment and retraining for when their short sporting careers are over. The thought that any traditional business would do anything like this is alien. Many companies do nothing at all. But Spedan Lewis did all this and more. He saw to it that doctors were employed in the workplace, as well as physiotherapists and chiropodists. To this day, you can still have your feet treated – it's £3 a foot! It makes commercial sense too: if you work in a job where you are on your feet all day, or involved in manual labour, the provision of these services keeps employees at work.

To acknowledge the stress caused by financial problems, Spedan set up a committee to help Partners with money issues, with interest-free loans and, if required, free independent financial planning. Free legal services were also made available. He encouraged the development of Partners' interests outside of work and would subsidise their hobbies, with Partners encouraged to set up a whole range of societies. I was initially drawn to the Partnership because of its five ocean-going yachts and two golf courses! Spedan's purpose was both to develop a more rounded individual and to encourage Partners to socialise together, creating greater bonds. The importance of holidays to well-being was recognised, and to this day the Partnership owns five country homes and holiday centres for Partners to stay at, with heavily subsidised rates. Vocational development came with a 100 per cent subsidy, cultural development with a 50 per cent subsidy for the theatre, concerts, opera, galleries and museums. Spedan wanted Partners to work for the Partnership for life, so six months' paid leave is given after twenty-five years' service to refresh and develop. To ensure Partners could retire with dignity, he introduced a pension scheme ahead of the state and helped retiring Partners plan ahead. All quite remarkable.

There are great examples elsewhere of a commitment to employee well-being. Unipart, for instance, which I will talk about later, demonstrate a passion to achieve the very highest health-and-safety standards, not only to show their employees that they care about them, but to reduce absenteeism and increase the benefits of training and thus productivity.

So many health and welfare problems today are caused by people feeling disenfranchised. They work for minimum wage, while most of those on zero-hours contracts don't even know what they'll bring home from one week to the next. They'll be told where to be and when and little else about the organisation they work for. It is little wonder they feel like they have no power or control over their working life, development or status, nor that these feelings of helplessness spill over into their personal life in the form of stress, depression and fatigue. They are not being treated well and they know it. They will certainly struggle to contribute to a company's success beyond the basics asked of them.

How can you be engaged in a company's success if you are a temporary worker on a zero-hours contract?

There is a growing body of evidence to support the idea that well-being is an essential aspect of employee engagement. It leads to improved production, lower rates of absence and stress, and higher levels of motivation. In other words, employee health and well-being has become a hard economic factor. Meaningful work leads to lower levels of absence because people are engaged and the association between meaningfulness and engagement is strengthened by well-being.[49] Those that are absorbed in their work are almost three times as likely to have six key positive emotions at work: enthusiasm, cheerfulness, optimism, contentment, a feeling of calm and being relaxed. We know from experience this leads to a better experience for customers and a stronger business proposition.

While most business leaders readily accept that a happy, healthy workforce is more productive, efficient and loyal, employee well-being and engagement often

[49] 'Creating an Engaged Workforce,' CIPD, January 2010.

seems to be an 'optional extra', rather than central to the way of doing business. Those companies that do recognise the potential impact still tend to be firmly in a responsive mindset when issues such as workplace stress arise, rather than planning ahead and looking towards more holistic, preventative strategies. Positive employee engagement is founded on creating an environment where employees are able to actively participate in workplace decisions and enjoy a sense of achievement with a job well done. Emotionally engaged employees, who connect with the values of their organisation, work harder and are far less likely to do anything that might damage the company they work for. None of the actions or strategies outlined in this book can be effective unless an employer creates the right environment in which employees can make informed, well-thought-through and prudent choices. To do this your team need to be relaxed, healthy and feel comfortable in their environment.

Health and well-being can be broken down into three key areas: physical, emotional and financial. By addressing all three, employers will improve engagement levels and productivity.

Physical health is often the first aspect of health and well-being that employers consider, but, even so, the signs are they are not doing a very effective job. Surveys show 43 per cent of employees do not feel their employers do anything to look after their physical health needs at work, whether it is encouraging the team to eat healthily, discouraging 'overwork', or promoting preventative health initiatives, such as flu jabs.[50] This figure rises to 55 per cent in some sectors, such as retail, catering, travel and transport, while a troubling 64 per cent of unskilled manual workers say their employer does nothing.

In the area of emotional well-being, it is interesting that employers often feel they are doing a better job than they are. In the UK 47 per cent of employees feel neglected, while just 13 per cent of employers felt they'd fallen down on the job. This could well be because facilities such as helplines, or face-to-face counselling, or an 'open door' policy are in place, but are just not

[50] 'Engaging Employees through Health and Wellbeing,' Simply Health, June 2011.

communicated effectively. Either way, there is a long way to go. There is certainly a need for employers to show more compassion in the event of personal issues and to make greater inroads on work-life balance. We have a duty to show we care. There are simple ways to do this: writing a personal note to an employee who has been seriously ill or had a bereavement in their family, for example. Or dropping a line to celebrate success when the opportunity arises. I often wonder why employees should be interested in what might be seen as their manager's success if their manager isn't interested in them.

In terms of finances, almost two thirds (62 per cent) of employees saw a need for their companies to provide help with their financial well-being, but felt this need was being ignored. By financial well-being we mean so much more than simply providing a wage for hours worked, or even a bonus scheme. This could encompass anything from childcare vouchers, to staff discounts, to financial education events to help workers manage their personal budgets or understand their pension entitlement. Getting into financial difficulties can have a really adverse effect on a worker's emotional state.

Business in the Community has done some sterling groundwork in developing its Workwell model, which guides companies through the practicalities of delivering a holistic well-being strategy. The idea behind it is to give companies practical assistance in creating an environment where employees can make informed choices and employers can support them in their aims. After all, pursuing a strategy of health and well-being is about prevention rather than cure.

The Partnership also thinks about health and well-being in the context of the working day. The drivers of well-being are as follows:

- Providing support and enabling good relationships, both among peers and managers, and encouraging positive behaviour.

- Ensuring jobs and the working environment are well designed. This doesn't just cover the roles themselves, but also the fact that workers are given the tools they need to do the job properly.

- Giving control and autonomy, because individuals desire a say over how they work, but also supporting them with clear feedback.

- Helping employees to find meaning and purpose at work, both in understanding the strategic aims of their organisation and what it means to them on a personal level.

- Providing support and opportunities for individuals to use their skills, strengths and talents.

Everyone plays a role in this, from the chief executive, to managers, to employees. Take managing stress as an example. We all need to work together to support everyone on the team and reduce stress. The person at the top of an organisation should lead the way by actively recognising and rewarding managers for supporting sustained well-being. Senior staff need to understand they play a part in the way they behave. Managers who pass on stress by panicking about deadlines, or who do not provide advice to staff, or even consult with them, can erode motivation and employee health and well-being.[51] The senior team should allow people a sense of control and help them understand that what they do matters. This needs policies and programmes in place to inform and educate at all levels on how to maintain psychological as well as physical well-being.

As well as being a strategy that works across all levels it is particularly important in large organisations, which may be spread over many sites. Managers in each individual unit need to sign up to promoting health and well-being as an integral part of development and performance management. A good example of how to respond to a dispersed workforce is to look at the approach taken by Deloitte which, alongside access to web-based information, created a network of champions who represent the well-being agenda in each

[51] 'The Business Case for Employees' Health and Wellbeing,' Steven Bevan, Work Foundation, 28 February 2010.

region across the UK. Their role is to raise awareness through local communication channels and events to equip their people to manage their well-being. Where they have a large concentrated population on their London campus, they've got an on-site gym, as well as a comprehensive health suite offering a range of support from a GP service and physiotherapy, through to occupational health and dental services. They also have a long-established group of mental-health champions based across the country, made up of partners trained to be able to offer confidential advice and support for any of their people suffering from stress or anxiety. Deloitte has put in place development programmes to help their people manage their well-being at key milestones in their career. These start with their new students, who need to understand about the importance of resilience techniques in order to sustain successful careers.

At the heart of well-being are relationships based on mutual trust and respect that managers have with their team members, and individuals have with one another, so they are able to proactively and reactively spot and discuss any concerns they may have and get the timely help they need. Listening to employees and responding to their anxieties plays a crucial role too. Everyone needs to feel they have a 'voice'. Experience in the John Lewis Partnership shows the main thing that exercises Partners is when they think the balance is wrong, in particular in relation to money or how they are rewarded for their work. Their efforts are recognised through a combination of pay, bonuses, benefits and in the pressure they feel at work. Contrary to the expectation that the majority will put money as the biggest driver, there is often a passionate debate among Partners over whether it would be better to lower the bonus rather than cut staff numbers in a tough year. Many individuals feel, quite understandably, they already work too hard and for too many hours. Trying to find the equilibrium is just as important to Partners as to management and they appreciate being asked to contribute to the debate.

CASE STUDY

Virgin West Coast responded to low engagement and high sickness levels in its organisation through its Good Together health and well-being programme. As well as reducing the average sickness absence per person from 13.7 to fewer than 8.6 days, which produced savings of £2.6 million through reduced absenteeism, the train operator improved its customer satisfaction scores to the highest level since 1993 and increased passenger numbers by 25 per cent and operating profits by 6.6 per cent.

The Good Together programme included health surveillance road shows and health kiosks to enable to employees to check weight, blood pressure, BMI and risk of heart disease. Health and well-being booklets were issued to all employees, and stress and well-being e-learning modules were made available 24/7.

Attending to health and well-being creates a virtuous circle of benefits. Not only is there a strong correlation between pastoral care and employee engagement, the two are mutually reinforcing. Healthy employees are more committed, and committed employees are more healthy. The feeling translates to all aspects of their lives too. Individuals who feel engaged and productive at work assess their overall lives more highly than those who are not engaged, or actively disengaged.[52] Since work is the primary activity for many of us during our waking hours, engagement truly does dictate the way we enjoy our lives. Or, as the saying goes: 'Choose a job you love, and you will never have to work a day in your life.' Engaged, healthy employees are also better equipped to deal with major changes or disruptions that occur in both their working and personal lives, which might otherwise throw them off course.

The focus here needs to be on the long term. Businesses that pursue a strategy of engagement in the short term, without thinking about well-being, won't be able to sustain the strategy. If you achieve high engagement, but suffer from low well-being, over time you risk burn out. There will be higher absence rates and a higher employee turnover, which will be ultimately self-defeating. The inescapable truth is that while engagement is essential for performance, that performance will never be exceptional, or sustainable,

[52] 'State of the Global Workforce,' Gallup, 8 October 2013.

without the health and well-being of your team. Individuals work most productively for sustained periods where there are high levels of engagement *and* well-being. It is, however, something a business needs to actively pursue. It won't just happen. Employee well-being is a cause of success, not simply a result of it.

There are wider benefits to the national economy too. A few years ago PWC produced a report say that sick absence cost the UK economy around £29 billion each year. It is suggested that 130 million days work are lost. Lower absenteeism and a healthier workforce will lead to greater productivity and increased economic wealth. More workplace health interventions lead to less demand on the National Health Service (NHS), which should lead to lower costs and better service for those most in need. I raised the contract between business and government at the start of this book. It should be mutually reinforcing, where business is helped to succeed and in return plays a greater part in society's well-being. Working together on health and well-being is a perfect example of a win-win. If the power of thinking in each area of government was turned to examining what was needed to help business to flourish, with an explicit expectation in return that business would play its part in public services, the country would be much better off.

Chapter eight

Step Five: Instilling pride

Making a difference is engaging

Pride is a powerful motivator. The feeling that what you do is worthwhile drives exceptional service, continued innovation and commitment. Think of companies famous for their exceptional service, such as Southwest Airlines, Disney, Virgin and, of course, the John Lewis Partnership. None of these throws money around to motivate employees. Apart from anything else, it is never enough. Yet each one has built its reputation through the pleasure its people take in working for the business. Pride is the motivation to be the best. Instilling pride is what enables us to get higher levels of performance from our people.

These businesses are the exception, though, not the rule. Just two-fifths of employees say they are proud to work for an organisation, and that figure is falling.[53] Meanwhile, just 22 per cent of employees felt good about their employer's behaviour towards society.[54]

Employees who love what they do and feel proud of where they work will speak openly and positively about it to colleagues, potential employees, customers and people in their community. When people ask that inevitable, getting-to-know-you question of 'where do you work', you'll hear the pleasure in their voice when they reply. Instilling such pride is not just about stirring speeches, sharing growth figures, or saying a few well-placed thank yous. It centres on having a purpose and helping everyone see that what they do each day is worthwhile. A big part of that is to do with how your business interacts with the wider world. People want to work for an organisation that cares about how it impacts on society. If they feel they make a difference, it leaves them more fulfilled. Thus, for example, Pets at Home won the *Sunday Times* Best

[53] 'Creating an Engaged Workforce,' CIPD, January 2010.

[54] Business in the Community/Ipsos MORI, April 2015.

Big Company to Work For 2013 and was ranked first by its employees for making a difference to the world (78 per cent), having re-homed 57,000 animals the previous year and raised £1.65 million for re-homing and animal charities.

Over half (57 per cent) of UK employees want their employers to do more for Corporate Social Responsibility (CSR) and 63 per cent say paid time off during working hours for charitable initiatives would significantly improve their engagement. It's not a 'like to have' either: 51 per cent believe their company has a duty to commit to charitable acts and CSR.[55] We are not talking here about a nod towards CSR, with a few big donations here, a sponsorship there and a self-congratulatory grin-and-handgrip photo of senior managers in the local paper. No, what is needed is a fully rounded strategy that focuses on giving, community partnerships, local involvement, philanthropy and employee volunteering. And it must be aligned to what the company is trying to achieve commercially.

[55] 'Towers Perrin-ISR Global Survey,' Towers Perrin, 2007.

There are still some who are suspicious of CSR. They question what it will do for their organisation and how encouraging employees to volunteer or engage in social or environmental activities will improve profitability. Well, it does. In fact, CSR plays a crucial role in employee engagement, with all the advantages of increased productivity, innovation and staff retention that goes with it. *Plus* it affords any company the opportunity to bring about a positive change on a mass scale. It doesn't just make sense for the business and your employees, but also has the potential to significantly impact on the wider society and change people's lives for the better.

To understand how powerful this can be, look at the example of two exceptional CSR initiatives. The first concerns pharmaceuticals giant GlaxoSmithKline (GSK), which was one of the first organisations to respond to the West Africa Ebola crisis that emerged in March 2014. As well as £450,000 of cash donations, the group provided products to the value of £770,000 and coordinated an extraordinary response of frontline health workers and volunteer experts. The initiative helped to keep supply chains open, so medicines could be delivered to patients, and contributed to the acceleration of the development of an Ebola vaccine. This was a perfect example of a large, skilled organisation using its expertise to make a huge difference.

In a similar vein, British Airways regularly mobilises its employees and resources to deliver life-saving relief for communities affected by major disasters, even organising flights to destinations not normally served by the airline. As well as providing valuable help where people need it most, each time the airline steps in, staff get the opportunity to develop skills by putting themselves in challenging situations. Therefore, in addition to boosting motivation, morale and loyalty, initiatives like these develop expertise in decision-making, problem-solving, project management and team-building. It also encourages, motivates and stimulates creative thinking and can even provide valuable networking opportunities through collaboration with other organisations. By working across their usual job functions, British Airways employees break down barriers, and work with and learn from experts.

There can be few employees who could fail to be motivated by such opportunities. What makes them even more powerful is when they are relevant and take advantage of the inherent expertise in each organisation, aligning with the business strategy as a whole. Where possible, it's best to tackle volunteering and charitable initiatives in areas that are most in tune to the skills and professional goals of your team. This delivers the dual benefit of adding more value for the charity involved and encouraging employees to learn new skills in a different environment. Thus a large IT service company might offer its services to help train underprivileged children or older people in tech skills. The IT experience will prove invaluable to the people being helped and, as well as pride in doing something worthwhile, the volunteers will get valuable feedback from the end-user. Barclays Digital Eagles scheme did just this, brilliantly helping elderly customers become IT literate and allowing them to access less-expensive-to-run online banking. A great win-win example. Get it right and it can be a dynamic way to bring corporate values to life, engaging employees, customers and suppliers.

My consistent experience has been that Partners valued and enjoyed activities like these and felt their contributions reflected the Partnership's core values. Waitrose is obviously in a strong position to add skills to a range of issues, from sustainable sourcing to fair trade, to healthy eating. This is why the Waitrose Way has made a significant difference internally as well as externally. The Waitrose Way pledges, which were launched in May 2013, were an opportunity to build on the successful Waitrose Way CSR policy launched two years earlier. The aim was to engage both Partners and customers in the simple ways they could live more sustainably. The four pillars of the Waitrose Way are:

- Championing British produce

- Treading lightly on the environment

- Treating people fairly

- Living well

We identified green energy and supporting regional or British food as two issues that resonated most strongly with both Partners and customers. In recent years, more and more consumers have wanted to know where their food comes from, how it is produced and how it gets here. We work hard to make sure people understand more about the way things get onto the supermarket shelves. Partners are integral to this strategy and take huge pride in sharing their knowledge with customers. The message is that small changes can have a significant impact on the environment, local communities and health.

For employees to perceive a company as responsible and a worthwhile place to be, the strategy has to be authentic, and they need to be free to fully participate at every level. Better still, the team should be able to lead programmes of events. Our aim is to involve as many people around the company as possible. CSR isn't effective – or fun – if only a few people do it. Sharing experiences among Partners, customers and the community improves motivation and engagement.

The Waitrose Community Matters scheme has

donated more than £14 million to more than thirty-eight thousand local charities chosen by customers between 2008 and 2015. Shoppers are given a green token at the end of every shopping trip to place in the box of the good cause they'd most like to support. The more tokens a cause gets, the bigger the donation. Since May 2012, this model was extended into Community Matters Partner Volunteering where local causes can bid for Partner time. Partners can choose their projects and do everything from painting a local playgroup wall, to helping out at a charity fun day. Partners are also encouraged to apply for six-month secondments at charities and are kept on at full pay. It all has a massively positive effect on the morale and well-being of the workforce.

CASE STUDY

Telecoms reseller Chess matches funds raised by employees up to £100 and gives them one paid day off a year for volunteering for charitable initiatives, from sponsored sky dives to 10k runs. The firm, which has 320 employees, raised £50,000 in 2014 for good

---

causes, including the Prince's Trust, Cancer Research UK and East Cheshire Hospice. It has also instigated a number of environmentally friendly policies, such as a cycle-to-work scheme, carbon offsetting and energy-saving schemes.

Volunteering is perhaps an area of CSR that has seen the most change in recent years. Once upon a time it was driven by a few passionate individuals, now it is an integral part of business for some organisations, and there is no doubt it plays a crucial role in creating a healthy, motivated and engaged workforce. In 2010 Business in the Community (the UK's largest business-led charity) launched Give and Gain day to encourage a national day of volunteering from its partner companies. Five years on, nearly nineteen thousand employees took part, making a real difference to hundreds of communities and providing clear proof that employees enjoy stretching themselves and being challenged. Such initiatives also publicly demonstrate a company's commitment to its local community, and 85 per cent of employees believe the perception of their company has improved as a result of volunteering.[56] Their pride is well-founded; 75 per cent of the public now believe it is either very important, or absolutely essential for companies to act in a responsible way.[57] Plus, if you need a firm business case, you'll be pleased to hear that 88 per cent of consumers are more likely to buy from a business that visibly acts to improve society.[58]

One of the best parts about high levels of corporate social responsibility is that the pride in the way Waitrose does things can be infectious. A few Christmases ago, one of the Waitrose turkey farmers was affected by an outbreak of avian flu and, as a consequence, there were far fewer turkeys. We wrote to our customers, apologised that we would be unable to supply the turkey they had ordered for the festive season and explained why. What was really touching was the

[56] 'Volunteering is the Business: Employers' and Employees' Attitudes to Workplace-Based Volunteering,' YOUGOV, December 2010.

[57] 'More than CV Points? The Benefits of Employee Volunteering for Business and Individuals,' The Social Market Foundation, March 2010.

[58] 'Employee Volunteering: Who is Benefiting Now?' CSV, 2013.

number of customers who responded by saying: give our refund to the farmer. I'm convinced this wouldn't happen in many other businesses. Through the close links Waitrose has with its stakeholders, long-term relationships, which look out for employees, farmers and customers, have been created.

CSR initiatives attract people and keep them engaged. They help create a positive working environment where people work hard because they *want* to, not because they *have* to. They are motivated by a sense of achievement and by doing something worthwhile. Being able to contribute to a cause while at work improves commitment to both the core job and to the company as a whole.

CHAPTER NINE

Step Six: Job satisfaction

*The people when rightly and fully trusted will
return the trust – Abraham Lincoln*

There are many elements to feeling satisfied at work,
but time and again, personal development and the
strength of your relationship with your line manager
are cited as key. I remember many years ago, when I
ran a John Lewis department store, being asked by the
then Chairman if I would become Marketing Director
of Waitrose supermarkets. I almost fell off my chair,
as I knew nothing about marketing or supermarkets!
I asked the very obvious question, 'Why me?' He
explained he had two options: to recruit externally to
find an experienced marketeer who didn't understand
the Partnership's culture, or train an internal candidate
who did understand the culture. I accepted and, true to
his word, the Chairman sent me to London Business

School and INSEAD to learn to be a marketeer. This move echoed Spedan's principle that, given an equal choice between an internal and external candidate, the former should always be favoured. Culture trumps other considerations. Pets at Home, which, as I mentioned earlier, won the *Sunday Times* Best Big Company to Work For 2013, fills 90 per cent of all promotions from internal candidates. As it is with customers, the best approach is to nurture and develop the employees you have, rather than chase new ones. Did you know that McDonald's restaurants estimate it costs £750 to hire a new recruit? What an incentive to look after the ones you have.

The inescapable theme of this book is that we have nothing of greater value than our people. High levels of employee engagement is the key to unlock organisational success. Happy employees equal a solid, successful and long-lasting business. But what makes people tick on a personal level? In other words, what makes workers happy and satisfied at work? More importantly, what can we, as business leaders, do about it?

Research shows that the two biggest drivers of satisfaction are 'respectful treatment' and 'trust between employees and senior management'.[59] Indeed, being treated with respect is the greatest driver for people choosing one company over another if they are presented with two identical job offers (92 per cent of people, in a situation where they had two identical job offers, would hold whether the companies treated employees with respect to be an important factor in their decision making).[60] And a poor relationship with your manager is often the biggest reason for leaving, no matter how great the brand. Forget all the perks, incentives, reviews and motivational tactics: treating people like people, with humanity, is what really counts. Satisfaction is about what companies are doing at a personal level to make people's lives better. Developing a culture of trust and respect and giving workers opportunities to learn and develop will make all the difference. If you want to create deep-seated loyalty

[59] 'Employee Job Satisfaction and Engagement,' Society for Human Resource Management, June 2015.

[60] Business in the Community/Ipsos MORI, April 2015.

among your team you need to show them you care and let them have defined autonomy. It is impossible to have pride in what you are doing if you are constantly being told what to do and how to do it.

Personal satisfaction is derived through training and development that recognises the whole individual. It is also down to softer benefits that create a nicer working environment, which can be as simple as a please and thank you. Spedan Lewis wrote that the food in the staff dining rooms should be so good that people who left the business would regret it each mealtime! At the restaurant chain Nando's they throw legendary staff parties from 11pm to 5am. When you are sent your offer letter they even include two Alka Seltzers! In both organisations the aim is to create a culture that employees don't want to leave.

When employees feel their company appreciates them, they exert discretionary effort to make their workplace an even better place to be. They willingly contribute to their firm's continuing success. They'll do whatever is necessary to get the job done and get it right. The deep emotional attachment and loyalty to their employer means they stay for longer. Add all these elements together and it creates an energised workplace.

CASE STUDY

John Neill, Unipart's chairman and chief executive, decided twenty-five years ago that the skills and capability of the team, combined with the manufacturer's values and culture, would be the only enduring source of competitive advantage. Employee engagement would never be a 'programme' for Unipart. It would become part of their DNA.

To Unipart, employee engagement means empowering, enabling and motivating employees to take ownership of their day-to-day work to solve problems at their own level. Unipart's approach is based on the belief that engagement is driven by day-to-day activities as well as personal ownership and control over an individual's own work.

Engagement activities are wide-ranging. All employees have a development programme, and leaders are required to show personal commitment

---

to the health, safety and well-being of the team. Employees have a voice and are able to participate in regular surveys and get-togethers to review results and identify problems. They also look at what they do right to better understand their strengths and how they can build on them. Any problems are recorded, tracked and visibly displayed, so employees can see progress.

The company also runs a number of health and well-being initiatives, such as smoking cessation programmes. These are specific to individual sites so that they answer needs at a local level.

It's not just feel-good stuff. Unipart identifies over £2 million a year in cost savings through employees and teams solving things at their own level. Clients have benefited too; productivity improvements of 30 per cent have led to savings of over £240,000 for one client.

Personal engagement starts right at the beginning, with your recruitment process. It is easier to train nice people than train people to be nice. Getting the right fit is very important. Look for people with the right attitude, who talk positively about challenges and outcomes. Stress that the interview is not to test their technical skills, which will be clear already, but a chance for them to be open about how they work so as to weigh up whether they will complement the team and be happy. When I ran the John Lewis department store in Cheadle, Manchester, we arranged for each prospective recruit to spend an hour or so working with the team they had applied to join. We then asked the team if they wanted the person to be recruited. The move created a sense of responsibility among the team to embrace their new recruits. For those who are offered jobs, it is very apparent, very quickly, whether they have the 'right stuff'. In the case of the Partnership, new recruits will either 'get it', or they won't. Those that do, stay, and generally for a long time. Many of those that don't, won't make it past the first three-month review because they feel the responsibility is too great.

The Partnership hires great people. This means it makes sense to train them extensively, empower them and reward them with more than other retailers might pay them. As a result, they strive to do what's right for each other and for customers. From the start, it is made clear to them that the culture is one of trust. For someone to feel happy in their job they must feel as though they are trusted to do it. Over-checking, rather than coaching, quickly leads employees to feel they are not competent, or worse still that they just cannot be trusted to do something well.

By contrast, in other companies there seems to be more and more time and money being spent on checking that people are doing what they should be doing, rather than investing in helping them be great at what they do (the checkers checking the checkers, a syndrome highlighted in chapter three). Much of this is in response to a spate of high-profile corporate scandals, such as Enron, Bernie Madff's Ponzi scheme and Libor manipulation, but since new ones seem to erupt every year it would seem that looking over shoulders is not really the solution. Despite a succession of reports and legislation, very little has changed. If we trusted and encouraged our employees to do the right thing, they would blow the whistle far quicker than any corporate sub-committee. In the Partnership, five

Partners are elected to the board for that very reason. Create a culture of trust and engagement and workers require little supervision and management direction because they are already doing what they need to do with enthusiasm, not just to meet, but to exceed goals.

I rather agree with Abraham Lincoln when he said he would rather trust and be disappointed than mistrust and be miserable all the time.

When the Partnership is working at its best, managers discuss with Partners what needs to be done and then let them get on with it. If necessary there will be a coaching conversation about the best way forward, or how well something was done, but the initiative very much remains with the Partner. It's a different mindset, but it is the mindset that nurtures, develops and increases the happiness of your team.

Hand in hand with not constantly looking over Partners' shoulders is flexibility. There is more concern about getting the job done than with precisely how, allowing autonomy and the chance to learn for oneself. Employees value flexible work practices. This flexibility fits perfectly with the pursuit of a good work-life balance, another central tenet of the Partnership. There is a genuine belief that individual commitment should be judged on the basis of results achieved, not upon the hours put in. Obviously Partners in shops need to follow set hours, but a culture of 'presentism' at head office is most certainly discouraged. It is not beneficial to any workplace when individuals feel obliged to be seen in work for long hours to impress management.

Likewise, although modern communications mean it is possible to send work emails and texts to colleagues at all hours, clear parameters on communications have been set out. Every manager in Waitrose has an iPad. When we first distributed them, we sent a note which said: 'there is no expectation that you will answer an email after 6 o'clock in the evening and before 8 o'clock the next morning'. That is their own time. If they choose to reply because they want to, that is fine. But we reminded them that just because they were happy to do so, they couldn't expect everyone else to do it.

Respect and fair treatment are crucial. As fellow owners in the Partnership, individuals respect each other whatever their positions. Managers naturally *invite* employees to participate in decisions. There are clearly defined organisational objectives so everyone knows where the business is heading and the goals for today, tomorrow and further ahead into the future. But for workers to feel truly respected, there has to be a strong commitment to their personal needs, as well as the needs of the business as a whole.

The Partnership model is geared towards encouraging individuals to pursue courses and learn new skills so they can rise up in the organisation or earn more in their role. It is so much better for morale when employees see clear advancement opportunities. Training is hugely important. When running department stores, I expected each full-time employee to do an hour of computer-based training or personal development a week. The desire is for Partners to be educated and developed in order to be intuitive interpreters of customers' needs.

Partners' career aspirations are listened to and taken seriously so they can be helped to satisfy their personal ambitions. It is a core part of their annual appraisal. Say, for example, a buyer is passionate about root vegetables. They'd be fully supported in that to ensure they become the most knowledgeable root veg buyer in the world, sending them back to college and around the world to fulfil this ambition. In most other businesses, that same buyer would be given a three-year term as a root veg buyer and then moved on in case they were getting 'too entrenched' with suppliers and no longer getting the best deal. Experience shows, however, that extensively trained and developed buyers can be just as competitive. They will also have an added pride in their achievement and status and will be better informed and able to do their job more effectively for both the company and the customer. People want to be recognised, to be part of something and to make a difference.

If you really care about the development of your people and believe that a more rounded individual can contribute more, it becomes logical to encourage their out-of-work hobbies and passions. In the John Lewis Partnership all vocational training is fully subsidised and, unusually, non-vocational training is subsidised by up to 50 per cent. Having helped develop the individual, the Partnership's aim is to pay as much as is warranted for their additional capability. Pay ranges stretch by up to 30 per cent at each level and through becoming a specialist, say in meat or fish, the range can stretch even further.

Similarly, everyone who works at Pets at Home has access to a wide variety of specialist training courses including pet nutrition, microchipping, grooming and the legally recognised Suitably Qualified Person (SQP) qualification, enabling them to dispense licensed flea and worm treatments. All of which means staff can develop, add more and earn more.

Employees must believe that what they do complements the greater whole. There are real benefits from spending more time showing employees how their individual contributions help their company succeed. Whether it is someone in purchasing who finds a way to improve the quality of products, or a cashier that sees to it a customer leaves with a smile on their face, it pays to communicate that these actions are crucial to corporate success. Be sure to celebrate successes and achievements. It doesn't take much to recognise a job well done, but it immediately creates strong bonds and a sense of pride. Everyone needs to feel valued and be provided with the opportunity to make a difference through his or her work. It is an ongoing process where contributions are regularly noticed and appreciated. People thrive on praise. Equally, individuals should feel confident they are in an environment that constantly promotes learning, creativity and growth.

Job security and stability are also hugely valuable drivers in the way people feel about their employer. Employees who feel their positions are insecure, inevitably put in a lot of effort to impress, but at the same time will be looking for the life-raft of alternative employment should things not work out well. They'll feel undervalued and disconnected from their organisation. If, however, your company's goal is to provide sustained employment because you value longevity, the atmosphere and outcomes will be distinctly different. That means a commitment to continually retraining the existing experienced workforce in new skills required, rather than losing them and hiring afresh.

Being in a rewarding and satisfying relationship means both sides taking notice of what the other has to say. No one wants to work in a business where they simply survive from day to day. We all want to feel excited about our working day and look forward to a bright future. Businesses will only ever achieve their full potential with the full support of their teams, through their sense of self worth and maximised potential.

Chapter Ten

Diversity

*How bland the world would be if we were
all the same*

In this book I have not explored the Partnership's commercial strategy, but rather how, through focusing on employee engagement, it can better create and deliver its strategy. There is, however, one other element to how the John Lewis Partnership sets out to operate that helps to create the conditions for successful growth and engagement, and that is its approach to a diverse workforce.

I'm not talking here in the first instance about gender, race or sexual orientation diversity, although I'll come to that, but diversity of views, knowledge and experience. Diversity has become a numbers game, all about hitting quotas and targets in order to present equality in the workplace. But the real benefit of diversity runs deeper than this and is imperative to commercial success, high performing teams and workplace engagement.

You see, to be at their best, teams need the broadest range of experience in order to make high-quality decisions that benefit ALL employees, customers and shareholders. It is because it makes your business better and happier that you should recruit from the broadest possible range of backgrounds, not because you have a quota to hit. And to make that work, managers need to explain that differences are welcomed for everyone's benefit.

The enlightened approach of the Partnership's founder, Spedan Lewis, to his workforce extended to equality and diversity. Rule 54 in the Partnership's constitution, the first draft of which was written almost one hundred years ago, states: 'The Partnership takes no account of age, sex, marital status, sexual orientation, ethnic origins, social position or political views.' Rule 56 goes on to say:

The Partnership encourages Partners to fulfil their potential and increase their career satisfaction in the Partnership, by: (1) promoting Partners of suitable ability; (2) encouraging changes in responsibility; (3) providing knowledge and access to training to help them carry out their responsibilities better; (4) encouraging their personal development and interests in fields not directly related to their work.

I can do no better to explain Spedan's personal forward-looking commitment to this approach than to quote from his book, *Partnership for All*, published in 1948. He explained:

I believe that at present the world wastes a vast amount of really valuable feminine ability and that the Partnership has gained heavily from the extent to which in making important appointments it has disregarded sex. At present (February 1948) the Partnership has one hundred and fifty posts that are already carrying four figure incomes and of these thirty-nine carry £2,000 a year or more. Of the former, thirty-four are held by women and of the latter, ten.

So even then, just three years after the end of World War Two, a quarter of the business's highest paid jobs were filled by women; extraordinarily progressive for the time.

What he went on to say in the same book made that achievement possible:

> In my own view the Partnership should be very careful never to over influence a married women against giving up business or towards coming into it or returning to it after some absence but, if she has a real wish to earn an income, I would make all feasible adjustments to develop her full earning power and to give her full scope.

In this regard, the Partnership aims to be flexible in its working arrangements. Recent examples include job-shares for female branch managers and embracing mobile technology so managers can work from home as well as in the shop or office.

Promoting gender and race equality is inherent in the way the Partnership does business. These days it is far from alone, and in this I would cite the wonderfully progressive Channel 4 broadcaster as the best I have come across from a large pack. But it is sobering to note that the Partnership, even today, has a much higher proportion of women working at senior management/ director and board level than many competitors.

Once a diversity of thought, experience and background has been assembled, the key is to nurture and encourage it. Through a focus on sharing information and empowering Partners, the Partnership should realise the maximum potential from the richness of its diverse workforce. In these ways the goal is to make Partners' lives easier and happier – the Partnership's supreme purpose.

Chapter Eleven

Measuring workplace happiness

What we measure we can manage:
measuringworkplacehappiness.com

If you accept the straightforward logic that engaged employees drive improved commercial performance through superior customer service and productivity, which in turns leads to great profitability, you will inevitably be drawn to how you measure happiness and employee engagement. Businesses are very good at measuring the profit part of the equation, together with measures which directly drive that profitability, such as items produced per person or customers served per hour, but perhaps less good at monitoring those things that drive employee engagement. And even if they do, one wonders if they rank at the top of the operational performance and profit statistics monitored.

So where to start? To what extent is measuring employee happiness an art or a science? From the outset of the John Lewis Partnership, the measurement of happiness was an art. An art in which, from the first day of joining, managers and managed are trained. There were and are no short cuts.

Let me explain. There are numerous methods used by the Partnership to obtain qualitative feedback, which, over almost a century, have led to the formation of a strong culture. Culture to me is best described as the sediment of past transactions, and over almost one hundred years a lot of sediment has built up. So how does it work?

Firstly, there are managers in the business who are independent and critical of management. This critical side of the business reports directly to the Partnership's Chairman and ensures that managers are abiding by the constitution and operating in the interests of Partners. The critical management is embedded in all areas and at all levels to collect and share information on a continual basis. The role of the critical managers is to be impartial and speak 'truth to power'. The responsibility of management is to openly listen to and accept the feedback and, as appropriate, act upon it.

Next there is the journalism. Weekly magazines are published for the whole Partnership as well as individual business units. These are not run and managed by the management but by the critical side so as to be impartial and open. Remarkably, the magazines welcome anonymous letters, often critical of management, which are an instant barometer of the mood of the organisation. A wise management acts upon them.

Then there is the Partnership's democracy. In Waitrose it is split over three levels: a branch council, then a regional council and finally a Waitrose council. There is then also a Partnership council. For each council, Partners run for election and through the successful candidates' terms of office they hold management to account and give feedback on how the business could be better – an invaluable source of information on Partner engagement and happiness. And to cap it all, five members of the Partnership Board are elected to post by their colleagues. Here, then, each month, is the chance for the most senior managers to hear how Partners are feeling.

As you can see, through all these channels there is no shortage of information, on a personal or business level, about the state of the business and Partner happiness. This is the art, and it takes time, particularly for new managers, to understand and embrace. So, to balance this, a number of quantitative measures are very helpful.

To begin there are a few measures that are relatively easy to collect. Four are key: staff turnover, sickness absence, internal promotions and longevity. Averages are often the preserve of the ill-informed and lazy, as while there is some advantage to understanding these figures on a company-wide basis, the real benefit comes in being able to break them down by department or manager. You see, employees will normally leave a manager who doesn't give them what they need, no matter how good the business or brand. As set out in the chapter on satisfaction, good line management is key to securing engagement. Enumerating the four statistics above is a good measure of how well line management is doing. I would wager that there will be a high correlation between the best commercial performing areas of a business and a manager with low staff turnover, low sickness absence and the greatest longevity of staff. I would further wager that in those departments, staff feel more valued and engaged. I wonder how many managers, though, have those three things at the top of their objective list, or the lead measure for any incentive payments?

It also pays to have a formal exit survey/interview to find out exactly what is driving the employee to leave. The information captured can then be circulated and used to help develop retention plans, reducing the considerable cost of recruitment, training and bringing new recruits to be optimally productive.

Lastly, an employee survey, whether annual or more frequent, will then add colour to the employment statistics. To my mind, the key to such an approach is not to use it to beat line management, but instead to inform and guide on how to improve staff turnover, sickness absence and longevity, etc., over time. Surveys are best, therefore, when consistent over a number of years, so as to monitor progress and build around the six areas crucial to achieve engagement, namely: reward and recognition, information, empowerment, well-being, worthwhile work and satisfaction. Within each of these areas each business will want to choose questions that are appropriate for them, but you could begin with a ten-question survey as straightforward as:

1. Do you feel appropriately rewarded for your work?
2. Do you feel recognised when you do something well?
3. Do you feel as though you have enough information to do your job well?
4. Do you feel empowered to make decisions?
5. Do you feel trusted to make decisions?
6. Do you feel the business cares for your well-being?
7. Do you feel you do something worthwhile?
8. Do you feel you are treated with respect?
9. Do you feel that you are being developed?
10. Do you feel satisfied in your work?

This sort of survey, scored on a 1–10, low to high basis, and coupled with employee comments, will provide the basis for building programmes for increasing employee happiness and engagement. You can visit measuringworkplacehappiness.com to see how you or your company score.

Afterword

There is a lot of finger pointing about the lack of trust between 'business' and 'society' – but who is society if not, to a large extent, the people working in business? And when we decry the 'short-termism' of the City and financial institutions, who among us has asked the people who manage our money to pay attention to factors other than maximising returns? If we haven't, surely we are just part of the problem? It is not 'the City' and those bad 'other' people – it is us!

To take a tangible example: the SABMiller board recently agreed to sell itself to ABInbev for £68 billion, one of the largest ever corporate deals. It is very hard to believe this deal will be good for customers, or the communities where the companies operate, or the employees of SABMiller. But the 2006 Companies Act invites directors to promote the success of their shareholders rather than stakeholders. To do otherwise would have seen uproar from their shareholders, who are very happy that they will do financial well having had the good sense or fortune to hold SABMiller's shares. And whose shareholding are these directors managing, but that of many good people who consider themselves compassionate capitalists?

The problem we face is not the distinction between good people, with a conscience, and amoral folk in the City and business, managing in a short-term manner without regard for the wider public good. Rather, it is that we have in place a system of directors and fund managers with legal and fiduciary responsibilities that requires certain types of behaviour. Without a change in these responsibilities, i.e., the law, or the law as understood, it is hard to see much changing, unless we, as shareholders and consumers and communities, reward those who behave sustainably in the interests of the many. Or unless directors and shareholders come to see the benefits of a more engaged workforce and the more sustainable approach to capitalism I have outlined. Ultimately it is about our humanity, our actions – that is where salvation lies. For this reason I have included the very relevant speech of Vaclav Havel, former president of the Czech Republic, to Congress in 1990 in the appendix.

But there is also a business rationale and response. I once asked Costas Markides, Professor of Strategic Leadership at London Business School, if there was one, fail-safe business strategy that has proved successful above all others. Without skipping a beat, he replied: 'Yes. It's doing the opposite of what others are doing.'

He's right, of course, and John Lewis Partnership's enduring success is predicated on doing things differently. What makes it all the more satisfying is that the people who work there believe it is doing the right thing too. They continue to fulfil the aims of the founder, Spedan Lewis, who said the Partnership was created wholly and solely to make the world a bit happier and a bit more decent.

There has never been a better time to spread this philosophy a lot more widely. Capitalism, globalisation and free trade are under threat. After a succession of financial scandals, stories of runaway shareholder greed, unethical behaviour, and abuse of monopoly power, trust in business and finance is at an all time low. The ordinary person on the street feels dispossessed and ignored, while to many it appears that the well-connected elite are running companies solely for their own benefit, with little reference to the needs of the community as a whole. Stories about the lack of tax paid by some corporate giants and individuals add to the frustration of families whose budgets are stretched to the limit.

The low turn-out at general elections among the younger generation, in particular, is said to be proof that they feel disenfranchised. It is a fact that they do not have many of the advantages of the previous generation. Many will struggle to get on the housing ladder, or get the jobs they expected after university. There is a view that it is only the people at the very top of society who see their pay and prospects expanding, along with those of their children. It is feared that a new generation is being created with little hope of any meaningful social mobility. There are many other countries where this problem is much more acute than here in the UK. The younger generation is making it clear it wants something different. Globally we see the rise of more extreme politics and so-called populist politics. People want a better life. The fact is that things need to change if we are to start re-engaging with them and so many others. All the signs are that we are at a pivotal point.

The answer, however, does not lie in revolution. All the evidence from history points to the fact that revolutions rarely work. People eventually kick back against dramatic and cataclysmic change and are resistant to lurching from one approach to another. Evolution, though, can be very successful.

I accept it is unrealistic to expect all businesses to convert to the John Lewis Partnership model of employee ownership, even though an increasing number are doing so. Apart from anything else, the system of public ownership is not broken; it is just not working in the best interests of everyone. However, I do believe there is an opportunity for more companies to reflect on some of the Partnership's advantages and work at improving employee engagement. It is in everyone's best interest: not only will it improve the lives of workers, but it will also be better for consumers, society and our communities. There is no reason not to do it from a purely commercial point of view, either, because as I have shown, this way of doing business has measurable advantages.

The Partnership Lite model referred to in this book is not one-size-fits-all. There will be aspects that suit some companies, yet don't work for others. It very much depends upon your culture and what you do. I talked in chapter six about having a framework that lays out the options for Partners before allowing them to get on with working out what works best for them. My obsession has always been with where we are going, rather than dictating how we get there, which leaves space to engage others to own the outcomes. I've done the same thing in setting out the six steps to employee happiness. Only you can say what works best for your organisation and how you choose to populate this framework. Each one of these steps makes a substantial difference, but the decision is yours on how important it is to make your employees feel better informed in your organisation, or the benefits of giving them more power and influence, or whether well-being should be the top of your priority list. I would very much hope that after reading this book managers will find ways to show individuals on their team that what they are doing is worthwhile, and help them have satisfying jobs.

This is not to say I would discourage any business from considering the full-fat, employee ownership model. I would certainly advocate a more diverse form of business ownership and believe if more businesses took this route it would make for a significantly healthier society, not just in terms of commercial success, but in terms of supporting the broader issues in society and narrowing the divide between the haves and have-nots. The government has lent its support to this idea by introducing two new tax incentives in 2014. And perhaps more could be done to promote wider share ownership by company employees. Whichever route you choose to take, what will underpin it all is strong leadership. It takes a special kind of leader, like Spedan Lewis, for these changes to happen.

Greater employee ownership or engagement might mean a huge leap for some businesses, particularly those that have traditionally had an overly directive style of leadership. We have become strongly immersed in this cult mindset that it is all about the individual running a company. It's the same in football, where managers are fêted and no one seems to notice their massive backroom staff. It is yet another sign of the narrowness in our thinking about who is creating the real value and whether or not it is being shared fairly and equally. Yes, a football manager, like a business leader, decides who is playing and in what formation, but it's the team and the people who support the team that dictate the success of the venture.

Engaging employees in a debate about how to do things better does mean you have to be more able to communicate effectively and take dissent more openly. Leaders must be prepared to accept that they are not perfect, and are never going to be, and then give their people a degree of freedom within the framework of their organisation. What leaders should be doing is creating a culture where lots of people deliver. The more people you can engage, the better the business will be.

However, giving employees power and information does not mean a leader doesn't have a crucial role both in decision-making and setting strategy. However switched-on the team is, there is no way companies should ask everyone, 'what do you think the strategy should be?' This will always be something that is decided upon at management level. The challenge and opportunity is then how you engage all your employees, both in understanding the issues and contributing to how they might best deliver the strategy. If you think you are leading people with equal responsibility and interest as you, your mindset is different.

At its best, your commercial strategy will reinforce employee well-being and happiness. In designing the commercial strategy for Waitrose, which we called VEG (Volume, Efficiency, Growth – with the wording very much dictated by being in the grocery trade), we put at its heart employee happiness. The idea behind VEG was to create a virtuous circle by increasing Volume from existing customers, driving Efficiency savings through increased volume and improved processes, leading to cash that can be invested in activities to Grow the business further. This increases Volume and the cycle is self-perpetuating. Taking it from a Partner viewpoint, Volume sustains employment, Efficiency enhances returns and Growth scales these returns and provides progression opportunities. Or, to put it another way: shareholder value is maximised in the long run by engaged employees giving great service with respect to suppliers and the communities where they work. When the goal is employee engagement, all else flows from that.

Tied up with this new approach is the need to shift to a longer-term outlook. The average tenure of a FTSE100 chief executive is now just five years. The longest-serving CEO has been in place since 1983, but for many the length of service is a fraction of this time. The message is clear: it is all about results, and if you don't get the right results for shareholders you are out. What sort of climate does that create? Certainly not one that acts in the best interest of the existing team.

Anyone who feels under this pressure will get rid of the existing teams and bring in their own people because they rely on a handful of people they trust to do as they are told. The company's culture is lost and valuable time is spent introducing a new one – repeatedly sometimes! Behaviour like this ripples down the whole organisation. It encourages people to cut corners and get results at all costs.

If we all acted like this we'd be doomed. The balance is all wrong. What has been discovered over many years in the Partnership is that employee happiness and a sense of ownership is good for the long term. Yes, there have been good years and there have been bad years. There are years when the Partnership is top of the pile and years when it is not. But if you take a long-term view, the Partnership numbers are really good. During that time any one of its rivals will have been flavour of the month for a while, as the Partnership very quietly plodded along. But, if you took a ten-year view, the Partnership would have done better than most of them. If investors were able to put money into the Partnership, they'd have done better in the long-term than with many of these other companies. A commitment to employee engagement is a commitment to long-term sustainability.

In the end, it all boils down to inputs and outputs. The prevailing thought in recent years has been that if you focus on making profit above all else, you get the best output. My response would be: but for whom and for how long? What Spedan Lewis realised a very long time ago is that if you look after your people you will get great output. Happiness is an input, not an output. We should be starting by trying to make people happy. If we get this right, everything else will follow: wealth will be more widely shared, the nation will become more productive and our communities will be better off. What I am calling for is for people to be more engaged in the workplace, to better share responsibility and rewards, engaged in the delivery of public services and engaged in our democracy. In short a more engaged society which promotes greater happiness, collective endeavour and fairer sharing of success.

What is being advocated here is more than making

a workplace, or even the world, a bit happier and a bit more decent. It's an argument in favour of a fairer form of capitalism because for capitalism to survive it needs to be more inclusive. Capitalism is not an end in its own right, it needs to be part of a value system. Smart societies cannot be created without fairness, equality and enfranchisement, and businesses have a crucial role to play. Society, quite rightly, expects a lot in return from business for the privileges it is afforded. Now is the time to deliver the goods.

Appendix

Set out below is the speech the newly appointed President of the Czech Republic, Vaclav Havel, gave to the Joint Session of the U.S. Congress shortly after the fall of the Berlin Wall and the 'Velvet revolution' in his home, Czechoslovakia. It is enlightening for two reasons. Firstly it sets out his views on what is required for the country to move from the strictures of communism. And secondly, it powerfully sets out the broader challenges a new world order would face.

A Joint Session of the U.S. Congress[61]

Washington, D.C., February 21, 1990

Dear Mr Speaker,
Dear Mr President,

---

[61] http://vaclavhavel.cz/showtrans.php?cat=projevy&val=322_aj_projevy.html&typ=HTML, retrieved on 29 January 2016.

Dear senators and members of the House,
Ladies and gentlemen:

My advisors have advised me, on this important occasion, to speak in Czech. I don't know why. Perhaps they wanted you to enjoy the sound of my mother tongue.

The last time they arrested me, on October 27 of last year, I didn't know whether it was for two days or two years. Exactly one month later, when rock musician Michael Kocab told me that I would probably be proposed as a presidential candidate, I thought it was one of his usual jokes.

On the 10th of December 1989, when my actor friend Jiri Bartoska, in the name of the Civic Forum, nominated me as a candidate for the office of the president of the republic, I thought it was out of the question that the Parliament we had inherited from the previous regime would elect me.

Twelve days later, when I was unanimously

elected president of my country, I had no idea that in two months I would be speaking in front of this famous and powerful assembly, and that I would be heard by millions of people who have never heard of me and that hundreds of politicians and political scientists would study every word I say.

When they arrested me on October 27, I was living in a country ruled by the most conservative Communist government in Europe, and our society slumbered beneath the pall of a totalitarian system. Today, less than four months later, I am speaking to you as the representative of a country which has complete freedom of speech, which is preparing for free elections, and which seeks to establish a prosperous market economy and its own foreign policy.

It is all very extraordinary indeed.

But I have not come here to speak about myself or my feelings, or merely to talk about my own country. I have used this small example of something I know well to illustrate something general and important.

We are living in extraordinary times. The human face of the world is changing so rapidly that none of the familiar political speedometers are adequate.

We playwrights, who have to cram a whole human life or an entire historical era into a two-hour play, can scarcely understand this rapidity ourselves. And if it gives us trouble, think of the trouble it must give to political scientists, who spend their whole lives studying the realm of the probable and have even less experience with the realm of the improbable than playwrights.

Let me try to explain why I think the velocity of the changes in my country, in Central and Eastern Europe, and of course in the Soviet Union itself, has made such a significant impression on the world today, and why it concerns the fate of us all, including Americans. I would like to look at this, first from the political point of view and then from a point of view we might call philosophical.

Twice in this century, the world has been threatened by a catastrophe. Twice this catastrophe was born in Europe, and twice Americans, along with others, were called upon to save Europe, the whole world and yourselves. The first rescue provided significant help to Czechs and Slovaks.

Thanks to the great support of your President Wilson, our first President, Tomas Garrigue Masaryk, was able to found a modern independent state. He founded it, as you know, on the same principles on which the United States of America had been founded, as Masaryk's manuscripts held by the Library of Congress testify.

At the same time, the United States made enormous strides. It became the most powerful nation on earth, and it understood the responsibility that flowed from this.

Proof of this are the hundreds of thousands of your young citizens who gave their lives for the liberation of Europe, and the graves of American airmen and soldiers on Czechoslovak soil.

But something else was happening as well: The Soviet Union appeared, grew, and transformed the enormous sacrifices of its people suffering under totalitarian rule into a strength that, after World War II, made it the second most powerful nation in the world. It was a country that rightly gave people nightmares, because no one knew what would happen and when to worsen the mood of its rulers, and what country it would decide to conquer and drag into its sphere of influence, as it is called in political language.

All of this taught us to see the world in bipolar terms, as two enormous forces, one a defender of freedom, the other a source of nightmares. Europe became the point of friction between these two powers, and thus it turned into a single enormous arsenal divided into two parts. In this process, one half of the arsenal became part of that nightmarish power, while the other the free part bordering on the ocean and having no wish to be driven into it, was compelled, together with you, to build a complicated security system, to which we probably owe the fact that we still exist.

So you may have contributed to the salvation of us Europeans, of the world and thus of yourselves for a third time: You have helped us to survive until today without a hot war this time, merely a cold one.

And now the totalitarian system in the Soviet Union and in most of its satellites is breaking down, and our nations are looking for a way to democracy and independence. The first act in this remarkable drama began when Mr Gorbachev and those around him, faced with the sad reality in their country, initiated the policy of 'perestroika'. Apparently they too had no idea what they were setting in motion or how rapidly events would unfold. We knew a great deal about the enormous number of growing problems that slumbered beneath the honeyed, unchanging mask of socialism. But I don't think any of us knew how little it would take for these problems to manifest themselves in all their enormity, and for the longings of these nations to emerge in all their strength. The mask fell away so rapidly that, in the flood of work, we have had literally no time even to be astonished.

What does all this mean for the world in the long run? Obviously a number of things. This is, I am firmly convinced, a historically irreversible process, and as a result Europe will begin again to seek its own identity without being compelled to be a divided armoury any longer. Perhaps this will create the hope that sooner or later your young men will no longer have to stand on guard for freedom in Europe or come to our rescue, because Europe will at last be able to stand guard over itself.

But that is still not the most important thing. The main thing is, it seems to me, that these revolutionary changes will enable us to escape from the rather antiquated straitjacket of this bipolar view of the world, and to enter at last into an era of multipolarity. That is, into an era in which all of us, large and small, former slaves and former masters, will be able to create what your great President Lincoln called 'the family of man'. Can you imagine what a relief this would be to that part of the world which for some reason is called the Third World, even though it is the largest?

I don't think it's appropriate simply to generalize, so let me be specific:

1) As you certainly know, most of the big wars and other European conflagrations

over the centuries have traditionally begun and ended on the territory of modern Czechoslovakia, or else they were somehow related to that area. Let the Second World War stand as the most recent example. This is understandable. Whether we like it or not, we are located in the very heart of Europe, and thanks to this, we have no view of the sea, and no real navy. I mention this because political stability in our country has traditionally been important for the whole of Europe. This is still true today. Our government of national understanding, our present Federal Assembly, the other bodies of the state, and I myself, will personally guarantee this stability until we hold free elections, planned for June.

We understand the terribly complex reasons, domestic political reasons above all, why the Soviet Union cannot withdraw its troops from our territory as quickly as they arrived in 1968. We understand that the arsenals built there over the past twenty years cannot be dismantled and removed overnight. Nevertheless, in our bilateral negotiations with the Soviet Union, we would like to have as many Soviet units as possible moved out of our country before the elections, in the interests of political stability. The more successful our negotiations, the more those who are elected will be able to guarantee political stability in our country even after the elections.

2) I often hear the question: How can the United States of America help us today? My reply is as paradoxical as the whole of my life has been: You can help us most of all if you help the Soviet Union on its irreversible, but immensely complicated, road to democracy. It is far more complicated than the road open to its former European satellites. You yourselves probably know best how to support, as rapidly as possible, the non-

violent evolution of this enormous, multinational body politic toward democracy and autonomy for all of its peoples. Therefore, it is not fitting for me to offer you any advice. I can only say that the sooner, the more quickly, and the more peacefully the Soviet Union begins to move along the road toward genuine political pluralism, respect for the rights of nations to their own integrity and to a working that is a market economy, the better it will be, not just for Czechs and Slovaks, but for the whole world. And the sooner you yourselves will be able to reduce the burden of the military budget born by the American people. To put it metaphorically, the millions you give to the East today soon will return to you in the form of billions in savings.

3) It is not true that the Czech writer Vaclav Havel wishes to dissolve the Warsaw Pact tomorrow and then NATO the day after

that, as some eager journalists have written. Vaclav Havel merely thinks what he has already said here, that American soldiers shouldn't have to be separated from their mothers for another hundred years just because Europe is incapable of being a guarantor of world peace, which it ought to be, to make at least some amends for having given the world two world wars.

Sooner or later Europe must recover and come into its own, and decide for itself how many of those soldiers it needs, so that its own security, and all the wider implications of security, may radiate peace into the whole world. Vaclav Havel cannot make decisions about things it is not proper for him to decide. He is merely putting in a good word for genuine peace, and for achieving it quickly.

4) Czechoslovakia thinks that the planned summit of countries participating in the

Helsinki process should take place soon, and that in addition to what it wants to accomplish, it should aim to hold the so-called Helsinki II conference earlier than 1992, as originally planned. Above all, we feel it could be something far more significant than has so far seemed possible. We think that Helsinki II should become something equivalent to a European peace conference, which has not yet been held; one that would finally put a formal end to the Second World War and all its unhappy consequences. Such a conference would officially bring a future democratic Germany, in the process of unifying itself, into a new pan-European structure which could decide about its own security system. This would naturally require some connection with that part of the globe we might label the 'Helsinki' part, stretching westward from Vladivostok and all the way to Alaska. The borders of the European states, which by the way should become gradually less important, should finally be legally guaranteed by a common, regular treaty. It should be more than obvious that the basis for such a treaty would have to be general respect for human rights, genuine political pluralism and genuinely free elections.

5) Naturally, we welcome the initiative of President Bush, which was essentially accepted by Mr Gorbachev as well, according to which the number of American and Soviet troops in Europe should be radically reduced. It is a magnificent shot in the arm for the Vienna disarmament talks and creates favourable conditions not only for our own efforts to achieve the quickest possible departure of Soviet troops from Czechoslovakia, but, indirectly as well, for our own intention to make considerable cuts in the Czechoslovak army, which is disproportionately large in relation to our population. If Czechoslovakia were forced to

defend itself against anyone, which we hope will not happen, then it would be capable of doing so with a considerably smaller army, because this time its defence would be not only after decades but even centuries supported by the common and indivisible will of both of its nations and its leadership. Our freedom, independence and our newborn democracy have been purchased at great cost, and we will not surrender them. For the sake of order, I should add that whatever steps we take are not intended to complicate the Vienna disarmament talks, but on the contrary, to facilitate them.

6) Czechoslovakia is returning to Europe. In the general interest and its own interest as well, it wants to coordinate this return both political and economic with the other returnees, which means, above all, with its neighbours the Poles and the Hungarians. We are doing what we can to coordinate

these returns. And at the same time, we are doing what we can so that Europe will be capable of really accepting us, its wayward children, which means that it may open itself to us and may begin to transform its structures which are formally European but de facto Western European in that direction, but in such a way that it will not be to its detriment but rather to its advantage.

7) I have already said this in our Parliament, and I would like to repeat it here, in this Congress, which is architecturally far more attractive: For many years, Czechoslovakia as someone's meaningless satellite has refused to face up honestly to its co-responsibility for the world. It has a lot to make up for. If I dwell on this and so many important things here, it is only because I feel along with my fellow citizens a sense of culpability for our former reprehensible passivity and a rather ordinary sense of indebtedness.

8) Last but not least, we are of course delighted that your country is so readily lending its support to our fresh efforts to renew democracy. Both our peoples were deeply moved by the generous offers made a few days ago in Prague at the Charles University, one of the oldest in Europe, by your secretary of state, Mr James Baker. We are ready to sit down and talk about them.

Ladies and gentlemen, I've only been president for two months, and I haven't attended any schools for presidents. My only school was life itself. Therefore, I don't want to burden you any longer with my political thoughts, but instead I will move on to an area that is more familiar to me, to what I would call the philosophical aspect of those changes that still concern everyone, although they are taking place in our corner of the world.

As long as people are people, democracy

in the full sense of the word will always be no more than an ideal; one may approach it as one would a horizon, in ways that may be better or worse, but it can never be fully attained. In this sense you are also merely approaching democracy. You have thousands of problems of all kinds, as other countries do. But you have one great advantage: You have been approaching democracy uninterruptedly for more than two hundred years, and your journey toward that horizon has never been disrupted by a totalitarian system. Czechs and Slovaks, despite their humanistic traditions that go back to the first millennium, have approached democracy for a mere twenty years, between the two world wars, and now for three and a half months since the 17th of November of last year.

The advantage that you have over us is obvious at once.

The Communist type of totalitarian system has left both our nations, Czechs and Slovaks, as it has all the nations of the Soviet Union and the other countries the Soviet Union subjugated in its time, a legacy of countless dead, an infinite spectrum of human suffering, profound economic decline, and above all enormous human humiliation. It has brought us horrors that fortunately you have not known.

At the same time, however unintentionally, of course it has given us something positive: a special capacity to look, from time to time, somewhat further than someone who has not undergone this bitter experience. A person who cannot move and live a normal life because he is pinned under a boulder has more time to think about his hopes than someone who is not trapped in this way.

What I am trying to say is this: We must all learn many things from you, from how to educate our offspring, how to elect our representatives, all the way to how to organize our economic life so that it will lead to prosperity and not poverty. But it doesn't have to be merely assistance from the well-educated, the powerful and the wealthy to someone who has nothing to offer in return.

We too can offer something to you: our experience and the knowledge that has come from it.

This is a subject for books, many of which have already been written and many of which have yet to be written. I shall therefore limit myself to a single idea.

The specific experience I'm talking about has given me one great certainty: Consciousness precedes Being, and not the other way around, as Marxists claim.

For this reason, the salvation of this human world lies nowhere else than in the human heart, in the human power to reflect, in human humbleness and in human responsibility.

Without a global revolution in the sphere of human consciousness, nothing will change for the better in the sphere of our Being as humans, and the catastrophe toward which this world is headed, whether it be ecological, social, demographic or a general breakdown of civilization, will be unavoidable. If we are no longer threatened by world war or by the danger that the absurd mountains of accumulated nuclear weapons might blow up the world, this does not mean that we have definitively won. We are in fact far from definite victory.

We are still a long way from that 'family of man'; in fact, we seem to be receding from the ideal rather than drawing closer to it. Interests of all kinds: personal, selfish, state, national, group and, if you like, company interests still considerably outweigh genuinely common and global interests. We are still under the sway of the destructive and thoroughly vain belief that man is the pinnacle of creation, and not just a part of it, and that therefore everything is permitted. There are still many who say they are concerned not for themselves but for the cause, while they are demonstrably out for themselves and not for the cause at all. We are still destroying the planet that was entrusted to us, and its environment. We still close our eyes to the growing social, ethnic and cultural conflicts in the world. From time to time we say that the anonymous megamachinery we have created for ourselves no longer serves us but rather has enslaved us, yet we still fail to do anything about it.

In other words, we still don't know how to put morality ahead of politics, science and economics. We are still incapable of understanding that the only genuine backbone of all our actions if they are to be moral is responsibility. Responsibility to something higher than my family, my country, my firm, my success. Responsibility to the order of Being, where all our actions are indelibly recorded and where, and only where, they will be properly judged.

The interpreter or mediator between us and this higher authority is what is traditionally referred to as human conscience.

If I subordinate my political behaviour to this imperative, I can't go far wrong. If on the contrary I were not guided by this voice, not even ten presidential schools with two thousand of the best political scientists in the world could help me.

This is why I ultimately decided after resisting for a long time to accept the burden of political responsibility.

I'm not the first nor will I be the last intellectual to do this. On the contrary, my feeling is that there will be more and more of them all the time. If the hope of the world lies in human consciousness, then it is obvious that intellectuals cannot go on forever avoiding their share of responsibility for the world and hiding their distastes for politics under an alleged need to be independent.

It is easy to have independence in your programme and then leave others to carry out that programme. If everyone thought that way, soon no one would be independent.

I think that Americans should understand this way of thinking. Wasn't it the best minds of your country, people you could call intellectuals, who wrote your famous Declaration of Independence, your Bill of Rights and your Constitution and who above all took upon themselves the practical responsibility for putting them into practice? The worker from Branik in Prague, whom your president referred to in his State of the Union message this year, is far from being the only person in Czechoslovakia, let alone in the world, to be inspired by those great documents. They inspire us all. They inspire us despite the fact that they are over two hundred years old. They inspire us to be citizens.

When Thomas Jefferson wrote that 'Governments are instituted among Men, deriving their just powers from the Consent of the Governed', it was a simple and important act of the human spirit.

What gave meaning to that act, however, was the fact that the author backed it up with his life. It was not just his words, it was his deeds as well.

I will end where I began. History has accelerated. I believe that once again, it will be the human spirit that will notice this acceleration, give it a name, and transform those words into deeds.

The Machine

by Mark Price

In the beginning was the idea and the idea was
good, so good it became a machine.

The machine only exists to make money for those
who own it.
The machine doesn't care about the consequences
of its actions if it makes more money.
The machine which hesitates is consumed by
another.
The machine doesn't mind being consumed if it
makes more money for the owners.
The machine demands consistency, order,
uniformity, process and efficiency.
The machine keeps making new rules and ways to
check them.
The machine doesn't trust
The machine gives orders but doesn't explain.
The machine talks to you but you can't talk to it.

The machine has to grow.
The machine demands more each year.
The machine which breaks down has its broken
parts reused or discarded.

There is a different way.

Publishing 2017

A heartwarming (and highly instructive) look at best practice
in business and how to learn from your mistakes.